HOLY MEN AND WOMEN OF THE MIDDLE AGES AND BEYOND

An Ignatius Press Reprint

Ignatius Press Reprints are identical in content with the most recent print edition of the original title. In order to keep important titles available at reasonable prices, we reprint them digitally in small quantities. We use high quality, acid-free paper, but the books are not smyth-sewn as is customary with our offset press print editions.

POPE BENEDICT XVI

HOLY MEN AND WOMEN OF THE MIDDLE AGES AND BEYOND

General Audiences

13 January 2010–26 January 2011

IGNATIUS PRESS SAN FRANCISCO

English translation by *L'Osservatore Romano*

Cover art:
Saint Francis and Saint Clare
By Giotto di Bondone (1266–1336)
Upper Church, S. Francesco, Assisi, Italy

Papal coat of arms image by www.AgnusImages.com

Cover design by Roxanne Mei Lum

Paperback Edition 2025

ISBN 978-1-62164-887-1
Library of Congress Control Number 2011924508
Printed in the United States of America ♾

CONTENTS

I

The Mendicant Orders

WEDNESDAY, 13 JANUARY 2010
Paul VI Audience Hall

Dear Brothers and Sisters,

At the beginning of the New Year, let us look at the history of Christianity to see how history develops and how it can be renewed. It shows that saints, guided by God's light, are the authentic reformers of the life of the Church and of society. As teachers with their words and witnesses with their example, they can encourage a stable and profound ecclesial renewal because they themselves are profoundly renewed, they are in touch with the real newness: God's presence in the world. This comforting reality, namely, that in every generation saints are born and bring the creativity of renewal, constantly accompanies the Church's history in the midst of the sorrows and negative aspects she encounters on her path. Indeed, century after century, we also see the birth of forces of reform and renewal, because God's newness is inexhaustible and provides ever new strength to forge ahead. This also happened in the thirteenth century with the birth and the extraordinary development of the Mendicant Orders: an important model of renewal in a new historical epoch. They were given this name because of their characteristic feature of "begging", in other words, humbly turning to the people for financial support in order to live their vow of poverty and carry out their evangelizing mission. The best known and most important of the Mendicant Orders that came into being in this period are the Friars Minor and the Friars Preachers, known as Franciscans and Dominicans. Thus they are called by the names of their Founders, Francis of Assisi and Dominic de Guzmán, respectively. These two great saints were able to read "the signs of the times" intelligently, perceiving the challenges that the Church of their time would be obliged to face.

A first challenge was the expansion of various groups and movements of the faithful who, in spite of being inspired by a legitimate desire for authentic Christian life, often set themselves outside ecclesial communion. They were profoundly averse to the rich and beautiful Church which had developed precisely with the flourishing of monasticism. In recent Catecheses I have reflected on the monastic community of Cluny, which had always attracted young people, therefore vital forces, as well as property and riches. Thus, at the first stage, logically, a Church developed whose wealth was in property and also in buildings. The idea that Christ came down to earth poor and that the true Church must be the very Church of the poor clashed with this Church. The desire for true Christian authenticity was thus in contrast to the reality of the empirical Church. These were the so-called paupers' movements of the Middle Ages. They fiercely contested the way of life of the priests and monks of the time, accused of betraying the Gospel and of not practicing poverty like the early Christians, and these movements countered the Bishops' ministry with their own "parallel hierarchy". Furthermore, to justify their decisions, they disseminated doctrine incompatible with the Catholic faith. For example, the Cathars' or Albigensians' movement reproposed ancient heresies such as the debasement of and contempt for the material world—the opposition to wealth soon became opposition to material reality as such—the denial of free will, and, subsequently, dualism, the existence of a second principle of evil equivalent to God. These movements gained ground, especially in France and Italy, not only because of their solid organization, but also because they were denouncing a real disorder in the Church, caused by the far from exemplary behavior of some members of the clergy.

Both Franciscans and Dominicans, following in their Founders' footsteps, showed, on the contrary, that it was possible to live evangelical poverty, the truth of the Gospel as such, without being separated from the Church. They showed that the Church remains the true, authentic home of the Gospel and of Scripture. Indeed, Dominic and Francis drew the power of their witness precisely from close communion with the Church and the Papacy. With an entirely original decision in the history of consecrated life, the Members of these Orders not only gave up their personal possessions, as monks had done since antiquity, but even did not want their land or goods to be made over to their communities. By so doing they meant to bear witness to an extremely modest life, to show solidarity to the poor, and to trust in Providence alone, to live by Providence every day, trustingly placing themselves in God's hands. This personal and community style of the Mendicant Orders, together with total adherence to the teaching and authority of the Church, was deeply appreciated by the Pontiffs of the time, such as Innocent III and Honorius III, who gave their full support to the new ecclesial experiences, recognizing in them the voice of the Spirit. And results were not lacking: the groups of paupers that had separated from the Church returned to ecclesial communion or were gradually reduced until they disappeared. Today too, although we live in a society in which "having" often prevails over "being", we are very sensitive to the examples of poverty and solidarity that believers offer by their courageous decisions. Today too, similar projects are not lacking: the movements, which truly stem from the newness of the Gospel and live it with radicalism in this day and age, placing themselves in God's hands to serve their neighbor. As Paul VI recalled in *Evangelii Nuntiandi*, the world listens willingly to teachers when they are also witnesses. This is a lesson never to be forgotten in the task of spreading the Gospel: to be a mirror reflecting divine love, one must first live what one proclaims.

The Franciscans and Dominicans were not only witnesses but also teachers. In fact, another widespread need in their time was for religious instruction. Many of the lay faithful who dwelled in the rapidly expanding cities wanted to live an intensely spiritual Christian life. They therefore sought to deepen their knowledge of the faith and to be guided in the demanding but exciting path of holiness. The Mendicant Orders were felicitously able to meet this need, too: the proclamation of the Gospel in simplicity and with its depth and grandeur was an aim, perhaps the principal aim, of this movement. Indeed, they devoted themselves with great zeal to preaching. Great throngs of the faithful, often true and proper crowds, would gather to listen to the preachers in the churches and in the open air; let us think, for example, of Saint Anthony. The preachers addressed topics close to people's lives, especially the practice of the theological and moral virtues, with practical examples that were easy to understand. They also taught ways to cultivate a life of prayer and devotion. For example, the Franciscans spread far and wide the devotion to the humanity of Christ, with the commitment to imitate the Lord. Thus it is hardly surprising that many of the faithful, men and women, chose to be accompanied on their Christian journey by Franciscan or Dominican Friars, who were much sought after and esteemed spiritual directors and confessors. In this way associations of lay faithful came into being, which drew inspiration from the spirituality of Saint Francis and Saint Dominic as it was adapted to their way of living. In other words, the proposal of a "lay holiness" won many people over. As the Second Ecumenical Vatican Council recalled, the call to holiness is not reserved to the few but is universal (cf. *Lumen Gentium*, no. 40). In all the states of life, in accordance with the demands of each one of them, a possibility of living the Gospel may be found. In our day, too, each and every Christian must strive for the "high standard of Christian living", whatever the class to which he belongs!

The importance of the Mendicant Orders thus grew so vigorously in the Middle Ages that secular institutions, such as the labor organizations, the ancient guilds, and the civil authorities themselves, often had recourse to the spiritual counseling of Members of these Orders in order to draw up their regulations and, at times, to settle both internal and external conflicts. The Franciscans and Dominicans became the spiritual animators of the medieval city. With deep insight they put into practice a pastoral strategy suited to the social changes. Since many people were moving from the countryside to the cities, they built their convents, no longer in rural districts, but rather in urban zones. Furthermore, to carry out their activities for the benefit of souls, they had to keep abreast of pastoral needs. With another entirely innovative decision, the Mendicant Orders relinquished their principle of stability, a classical principle of ancient monasticism, opting for a different approach. Friars

Minor and Preachers traveled with missionary zeal from one place to another. Consequently, they organized themselves differently in comparison with the majority of monastic Orders. Instead of the traditional autonomy that every monastery enjoyed, they gave greater importance to the Order as such and to the Superior General, as well as to the structure of the Provinces. Thus the Mendicants were more available to the needs of the universal Church. Their flexibility enabled them to send out the most suitable friars on specific missions, and the Mendicant Orders reached North Africa, the Middle East, and Northern Europe. With this adaptability, their missionary dynamism was renewed.

The cultural transformations taking place in that period constituted another great challenge. New issues enlivened the discussion in the universities that came into being at the end of the twelfth century. Minors and Preachers did not hesitate to take on this obligation. As students and professors, they entered the most famous universities of the time, set up study centers, produced texts of great value, gave life to true and proper schools of thought, were protagonists of scholastic theology in its best period, and had an important effect on the development of thought. The greatest thinkers, Saint Thomas Aquinas and Saint Bonaventure, were Mendicants who worked precisely with this dynamism of the new evangelization which also renewed the courage of thought, of the dialogue between reason and faith. Today, too, a "charity of and in the truth" exists, an "intellectual charity" that must be exercised to enlighten minds and to combine faith with culture. The dedication of the Franciscans and Dominicans in the medieval universities is an invitation, dear faithful, to make ourselves present in the places where knowledge is formulated so as to focus the light of the Gospel, with respect and conviction, on the fundamental questions that concern Man, his dignity, and his eternal destiny. Thinking of the role of the Franciscans and the Dominicans in the Middle Ages, of the spiritual renewal they inspired, and of the breath of new life they communicated in the world, a monk said: "At that time the world was aging. Two Orders were born in the Church whose youth they renewed like that of an eagle" (Burchard of Ursperg, *Chronicon*).

Dear brothers and sisters, at the very beginning of this year, let us invoke the Holy Spirit, the eternal youth of the Church: may he make each one aware of the urgent need to offer a consistent and courageous Gospel witness so that there may always be saints who make the Church resplendent, like a bride, ever pure and beautiful, without spot or wrinkle, who can attract the world irresistibly to Christ and to his salvation.

2

Saint Francis of Assisi

WEDNESDAY, 27 JANUARY 2010
Paul VI Audience Hall

Dear Brothers and Sisters,

In a recent Catechesis, I illustrated the providential role the Orders of Friars Minor and the Order of Preachers, founded by Saint Francis of Assisi and Saint Dominic de Guzmán respectively, played in the renewal of the Church in their day. Today I would like to present to you the figure of Francis, an authentic "giant" of holiness, who continues to fascinate a great many people of all age groups and every religion.

"A sun was born into the world." With these words, in the Divine Comedy (*Paradiso*, Canto XI), the great Italian poet Dante Alighieri alludes to Francis' birth, which took place in Assisi either at the end of 1181 or at the beginning of 1182. As part of a rich family—his father was a cloth merchant—Francis lived a carefree adolescence and youth, cultivating the chivalrous ideals of the time. At age twenty, he took part in a military campaign and was taken prisoner. He became ill and was freed. After his return to Assisi, a slow process of spiritual conversion began within him, which brought him gradually to abandon the worldly lifestyle that he had adopted thus far. The famous episodes of Francis' meeting with the leper to whom, dismounting from his horse, he gave the kiss of peace and of the message from the Crucifix in the small Church of Saint Damian date back to this period. Three times Christ on the Cross came to life and told him: "Go, Francis, and repair my Church in ruins." This simple occurrence of the word of God heard in the Church of Saint Damian contains a profound symbolism. At that moment Saint Francis was called to repair the small church, but the ruinous state of the building was a symbol of the dramatic and disquieting situation of the Church herself. At that time the Church had a superficial faith which did not shape or transform life, a scarcely zealous clergy, and a chilling of love. It was an interior destruction of the Church which also brought a decomposition of unity, with the birth of heretical movements. Yet, there at the center of the Church in ruins was the Crucified Lord, and he spoke: he called for renewal; he called Francis to the manual labor of repairing the small Church of Saint Damian, the symbol of a much deeper call to renew Christ's own Church, with her radicality of faith and her loving enthusiasm for Christ. This event, which probably happened in 1205, calls to mind another similar occurrence which took place in 1207: Pope Innocent III's dream. In it, he saw the Basilica of Saint John Lateran, the mother of all churches, collapsing and one small and insignificant religious brother supporting the church on his shoulders to prevent it from falling. On the one hand, it is interesting to note that it is not the Pope who was helping to prevent the church from collapsing but, rather, a small and insignificant brother, whom the Pope recognized in Francis when he later came to visit. Innocent III was a powerful Pope who had a great theological formation and great political influence; nevertheless, it was not he but the small, insignificant religious who was to renew the Church. It was Saint Francis, called by God. On the other hand, however, it is important to note that Saint Francis does not renew the Church without or in opposition to the Pope, but only in communion with him. The two realities go together: the Successor of Peter, the Bishops, the Church founded on the succession of the Apostles, and the new charism that the Holy Spirit brought to life at that time for the Church's renewal. Authentic renewal grew from these together.

Let us return to the life of Saint Francis. When his father, Bernardone, reproached him for being too generous to the poor, Francis, standing before the Bishop of Assisi, in a symbolic gesture, stripped off his clothes, thus showing he renounced his paternal inheritance. Just as at the moment of creation, Francis had nothing, only the life that God gave him, into whose hands he delivered himself. He then lived as a hermit, until, in 1208, another fundamental step in his journey of conversion took place. While listening to a passage from the Gospel of Matthew—Jesus' discourse to the Apostles whom he sent out on mission—Francis felt called to live in poverty and dedicate himself to preaching. Other companions joined him, and in 1209 he traveled to Rome, to propose to Pope Innocent III the plan for a new form of Christian life. He received a fatherly welcome from that great Pontiff, who, enlightened by the Lord, perceived the divine origin of the movement inspired by Francis. The *Poverello* of Assisi understood that every charism as a gift of the Holy Spirit existed to serve the Body of Christ, which is the Church; therefore he always acted in full communion with the ecclesial authorities. In the life of the saints there is no contradiction between prophetic charism and the charism of governance, and if tension arises, they know to await patiently the times determined by the Holy Spirit.

Actually, several nineteenth-century and also twentieth-century historians have sought to construct a so-called historical Francis, behind the traditional depiction of the Saint, just as they sought to create a so-called historical Jesus behind the Jesus of the Gospels. This historical Francis would not have been a man of the Church but, rather, a man connected directly and solely to Christ, a man who wanted to bring about a renewal of the People of God, without canonical forms or hierarchy. The truth is that Saint Francis really did have an extremely intimate relationship with Jesus and with the word of God, which he wanted to pursue *sine glossa*: just as it is, in all its radicality and truth. It is also true that initially he did not intend to create an Order with the necessary canonical forms. Rather, he simply wanted, through the word of God and the presence of the Lord, to renew the People of God, to call them back to listening to the word and to literal obedience to Christ. Furthermore, he knew that Christ was never "mine" but is always "ours", that "I" cannot possess Christ, that "I" cannot rebuild in opposition to the Church, her will, and her teaching. Instead, it is only in communion with the Church built on the Apostolic succession that obedience, too, to the word of God can be renewed.

It is also true that Francis had no intention of creating a new Order, but solely that of renewing the People of God for the Lord who comes. He understood, however, through suffering and pain that everything must have its own order and that the law of the Church is necessary to give shape to renewal. Thus he placed himself fully, with his heart, in communion with the Church, with the Pope, and with the Bishops. He always knew that the center of the Church is the Eucharist, where the Body of Christ and his Blood are made present through the priesthood, the Eucharist, and the communion of the Church. Wherever the priesthood and the Eucharist and the Church come together, it is there alone that the word of God also dwells. The real historical Francis was the Francis of the Church, and precisely in this way he continues to speak to non-believers and believers of other confessions and religions as well.

Francis and his friars, who were becoming ever more numerous, established themselves at the Portiuncula, or the Church of Santa Maria degli Angeli, the sacred place par excellence of Franciscan spirituality. Clare, too, a young woman of Assisi from a noble family, followed the school of Francis. This became the origin of the Second Franciscan Order, that of the Poor Clares, another experience destined to produce outstanding figures of sainthood in the Church.

Innocent III's Successor, Pope Honorius III, with his Bull *Cum Dilecti* in 1218 supported the unique development of the first Friars Minor, who started missions in different European countries and even in Morocco. In 1219 Francis obtained permission to visit and speak to the Muslim sultan Malik al-Klmil, to preach the Gospel of Jesus there, too. I would like to highlight this episode in Saint Francis' life, which is very timely. In an age when there was a conflict underway between Christianity and Islam, Francis, intentionally armed only with his faith and personal humility, traveled the path of dialogue effectively. The chronicles tell us that he was given a benevolent welcome and a cordial reception by the Muslim Sultan. It provides a model which should inspire today's relations between Christians and Muslims: to promote a sincere dialogue, in reciprocal respect and mutual understanding (cf. *Nostra Aetate*, no. 3). It appears that later, in 1220, Francis visited the Holy Land, thus sowing a seed that would bear much fruit: his spiritual sons would in fact make of the Sites where Jesus lived a privileged space for their mission. It is with gratitude that I think today of the great merits of the Franciscan Custody of the Holy Land.

On his return to Italy, Francis turned over the administration of his Order to his vicar, Brother Pietro Cattani, while the Pope entrusted the rapidly growing Order's protection to Cardinal Ugolino, the future Supreme Pontiff Gregory IX. For his part, the Founder, dedicated completely to his preaching, which he carried out with great success, compiled his Rule, which was then approved by the Pope.

In 1224, at the hermitage in La Verna, Francis had a vision of the Crucified Lord in the form of a seraph and from that encounter with the crucified seraph received the stigmata, thus becoming one with the Crucified Christ. It was a gift, therefore, that expressed his intimate identification with the Lord.

The death of Francis—his *transitus*—occurred on the evening of 3 October 1226, in the Portiuncula. After having blessed his spiritual children, he died, lying on the bare earthen floor. Two years later, Pope Gregory IX entered him in the roll of saints. A short time after, a great basilica in his honor was constructed in Assisi, still today an extremely popular pilgrim destination. There pilgrims can venerate the Saint's tomb and take in the frescoes by Giotto, an artist who has magnificently illustrated Francis' life.

It has been said that Francis represents an *alter Christus*, that he was truly a living icon of Christ. He has also been called "the brother of Jesus". Indeed, this was his ideal: to be like Jesus, to contemplate Christ in the Gospel, to love him intensely, and to imitate his virtues. In particular, he wished to give a fundamental values to interior and exterior poverty, which he also taught to his spiritual sons. The first Beatitude of the Sermon on the Mount—"Blessed are the poor in spirit, for theirs is the kingdom of heaven" (Mt 5:3)—found a luminous fulfillment in the life and words of Saint Francis. Truly, dear friends, the saints are the best interpreters of the Bible. As they incarnate the word of God in their own lives, they make it more captivating than ever, so that it really speaks to us. The witness of Francis, who loved poverty as a means to follow Christ with dedication and total freedom, continues to be for us, too, an invitation to cultivate interior poverty in order to grow in our trust of God by adopting also a sober lifestyle and a detachment from material goods.

Francis' love for Christ expressed itself in a special way in the adoration of the Blessed Sacrament of the Eucharist. In the *Fonti Francescane* (writings of Saint Francis) one reads such moving expressions as: "Let everyone be struck with fear, let the whole world tremble, and let the heavens exult, when Christ, the Son of the living God, is present on the altar in the hands of a priest. O stupendous dignity! O humble sublimity, that the Lord of the universe, God and the Son of God, so humbles himself that for our salvation he hides himself under an ordinary piece of bread" (Francis of Assisi, *Scritti*, Editrici Francescane, Padua, 2002, p. 401).

In this Year for Priests, I would also like to recall a piece of advice that Francis gave to priests: "When they wish to celebrate Mass, being pure, they offer the true Sacrifice of the most holy Body and Blood of our Lord Jesus Christ with purity and reverence" (Francis of Assisi, *Scritti*, p. 399). Francis always showed great deference toward priests and asserted that they should always be treated with respect, even in cases where they might be somewhat unworthy personally. The reason he gave for this profound respect was that they receive the gift of consecrating the Eucharist. Dear brothers in the priesthood, let us never forget this teaching: the holiness of the Eucharist appeals to us to be pure, to live in a way that is consistent with the mystery we celebrate.

From love for Christ stems love for others and also for all God's creatures. This is yet another characteristic trait of Francis' spirituality: the sense of universal brotherhood and love for creation, which inspired the famous *Canticle of Creatures*. This, too, is an extremely timely message. As I recalled in my recent Encyclical *Caritas in Veritate*, development is sustainable only when it respects creation and does not damage the environment (cf. nos. 48–52), and in the Message for the World Day of Peace this year, I also underscored that even building stable peace is linked to respect for creation. Francis reminds us that the wisdom and benevolence of the Creator is expressed through creation. He understood nature as a language in which God speaks to us, in which reality becomes clear, and we can speak *of* God and *with* God.

Dear friends, Francis was a great saint and a joyful man. His simplicity, his humility, his faith, his love for Christ, his goodness toward every man and every woman, brought him gladness in every circumstance. Indeed, there subsists an intimate and indissoluble relationship between holiness and joy. A French writer once wrote that there is only one sorrow in the world: not to be saints, that is, not to be near to God. Looking at the testimony of Saint Francis, we understand that this is the secret of true happiness: to become saints, close to God!

May the Virgin, so tenderly loved by Francis, obtain this gift for us. Let us entrust ourselves to her with the words of the *Poverello* of Assisi himself: "Blessed Virgin Mary, no one like you among women has ever been born in the world, daughter and handmaid of the Most High King and heavenly Father, Mother of our Most Blessed Lord Jesus Christ, spouse of the Holy Spirit. Pray for us . . . to your most blessed and beloved Son, Lord, and Master" (Francis of Assisi, *Scritti*, p. 163).

3

Saint Dominic Guzmán

WEDNESDAY, 3 FEBRUARY 2010
Paul VI Audience Hall

Dear Brothers and Sisters,

Last week I presented the luminous figure of Francis of Assisi; today I want to talk about another saint of the same period who made a fundamental contribution to the renewal of the Church of his time: Saint Dominic, the Founder of the Order of Preachers, also known as Dominican Friars.

His successor at the head of the Order, Blessed Jordan of Saxony, gives a complete picture of Saint Dominic in the text of a famous prayer: "Your strong love burned with heavenly fire and God-like zeal. With all the fervor of an impetuous heart and with an avowal of perfect poverty, you spent your whole self in the cause of the Apostolic life" and in preaching the Gospel. It is precisely this fundamental trait of Dominic's witness that is emphasized: he always spoke *with* God and *of* God. Love for the Lord and for neighbor, the search for God's glory and the salvation of souls in the lives of saints always go hand in hand.

Dominic was born at Caleruega, Spain, in about 1170. He belonged to a noble family of Old Castile and, supported by a priest uncle, was educated at a famous school in Palencia. He distinguished himself straightaway by his interest in the study of Sacred Scripture and by his love of the poor, to the point of selling books, which in his time were a very valuable asset, in order to support famine victims with the proceeds.

Ordained a priest, he was elected canon of the Cathedral Chapter in Osma, his native diocese. Although he may well have thought that this appointment might bring him a certain amount of prestige in the Church and in society, he viewed it, not as a personal privilege or as the beginning of a brilliant ecclesiastical career, but, rather, as a service to carry out with dedication and humility. Are not a career and power temptations from which not even those who have a role of guidance and governance in the Church are exempt? I recalled this a few months ago during the consecration of several Bishops: "We do not seek power, prestige, or esteem for ourselves.... We know how in civil society and often also in the Church things suffer because many people on whom responsibility has been conferred work for themselves rather than for the community" (16 September 2009).

The Bishop of Osma, a true and zealous Pastor whose name was Didacus, soon spotted Dominic's spiritual qualities and wanted to avail himself of his collaboration. Together they went to Northern Europe on the diplomatic missions entrusted to them by the King of Castile. On his travels Dominic became aware of two enormous challenges for the Church of his time: the existence of people who were not yet evangelized on the northern boundaries of the European Continent, and the religious schism that undermined Christian life in the South of France, where the activity of certain heretical groups was creating a disturbance and distancing people from the truth of the faith. So it was that missionary action for those who did not know the light of the Gospel and the work of the re-evangelization of Christian communities became the apostolic goals that Dominic resolved to pursue.

It was the Pope, to whom the Bishop Didacus and Dominic went to seek advice, who asked Dominic to devote himself to preaching to the Albigensians, a heretical group which upheld a dualistic conception of reality, that is, with two equally powerful creator principles, Good and Evil. This group consequently despised matter as coming from the principle of evil. They even refused marriage and went to the point of denying the Incarnation of Christ and the sacraments, in which the Lord "touches" us through matter, and the resurrection of bodies. The Albigensians esteemed the poor and austere life—in this regard they were even exemplary—and criticized the riches of the clergy of that time. Dominic enthusiastically accepted this mission and carried it out with the example of his own poor and austere existence, Gospel preaching, and public discussions. He devoted the rest of his life to this mission of preaching the Good News. His sons were also to make Saint Dominic's other dreams come true: the mission *ad gentes*, that is, to those who did not yet know Jesus, and the mission to those who lived in the cities, especially the university cities, where the new intellectual trends were a challenge to the faith of the cultured.

This great Saint reminds us that in the heart of the Church a missionary fire must always burn. It must be a constant incentive to make the first proclamation of the Gospel and, wherever necessary, a new evangelization. Christ, in fact, is the most precious good that the men and women of every time and every place have the right to know and love! And it is comforting to see that in the Church today, too, there are many—pastors and lay faithful alike, members of ancient religious orders and new ecclesial movements—who spend their lives joyfully for this supreme ideal, proclaiming and witnessing to the Gospel!

Many other men then joined Dominic de Guzmán, attracted by the same aspiration. In this manner, after the first foundation in Toulouse, the Order of Preachers gradually came into being. Dominic in fact, in perfect obedience to the directives of the Popes of his time, Innocent III and Honorius III, used the ancient Rule of Saint Augustine, adapting it to the needs of apostolic life that led him and his companions to preach as they traveled from one place to another but then returned to their own convents and places of study, to prayer and community life. Dominic wanted to give special importance to two values he deemed indispensable for the success of the evangelizing mission: community life in poverty and study.

First of all, Dominic and the Friars Preachers presented themselves as mendicants, that is, without vast estates to be administered. This element made them more available for study and itinerant preaching and constituted a practical witness for the people. The internal government of the Dominican convents and provinces was structured on the system of chapters which elected their own superiors, who were subsequently confirmed by the major superiors; thus it was an organization that stimulated fraternal life and the responsibility of all the members of the community, demanding strong personal convictions. The choice of this system was born precisely from the fact that as preachers of the truth of God, the Dominicans had to be consistent with what they proclaimed. The truth studied and shared in charity with the brethren is the deepest foundation of joy. Blessed Jordan of Saxony said of Saint Dominic: "All men were swept into the embrace of his charity, and, in loving all, he was beloved by all.... He claimed it his right to rejoice with the joyful and to weep with the sorrowful" (*Libellus de principiis Ordinis Praedicatorum autore Iordano de Saxonia*, ed. H. C. Scheeben, *Monumenta Historica Sancti Patris Nostri Dominici*, Rome, 1935).

Secondly, with a courageous gesture, Dominic wanted his followers to acquire a sound theological training and did not hesitate to send them to the universities of the time, even though a fair number of clerics viewed these cultural institutions with distrust. The Constitutions of the Order of Preachers give great importance to study as a preparation for the apostolate. Dominic wanted his friars to devote themselves to it without reserve, with diligence, and with piety; a study based on the soul of all theological knowledge, that is, on Sacred Scripture, and respectful of the questions asked by reason. The development of culture requires those who carry out the ministry of the Word at various levels to be well trained. I therefore urge all those, pastors and lay people alike, to cultivate this "cultural dimension" of faith, so that the beauty of the Christian truth may be better understood and faith may be truly nourished, reinforced, and also defended. In this Year for Priests, I ask seminarians and priests to esteem the spiritual value of study. The quality of the priestly ministry also depends on the generosity with which one applies oneself to the study of the revealed truths.

Dominic, who wished to found a religious order of theologian-preachers, reminds us that theology has a spiritual and pastoral dimension that enriches the soul and life. Priests, the consecrated, and also all the faithful may find profound "inner joy" in contemplating the beauty of the truth that comes from God, a truth that is ever timely and ever alive. Moreover, the motto of the Friars Preachers—*contemplata aliis tradere*—helps us to discover a pastoral yearning in the contemplative study of this truth because of the need to communicate to others the fruit of one's own contemplation.

When Dominic died in 1221 in Bologna, the city that declared him its Patron, his work had already had widespread success. The Order of Preachers, with the Holy See's support, had spread to many countries in Europe for the benefit of the whole Church. Dominic was canonized in 1234, and it is he himself who, with his holiness, points out to us two indispensable means for making apostolic action effective. In the very first place is Marian devotion, which he fostered tenderly and left as a precious legacy to his spiritual sons, who, in the history of the Church, have had the great merit of disseminating the prayer of the Holy Rosary, so dear to the Christian people and so rich in Gospel values: a true school of faith and piety. In the second place, Dominic, who cared for several women's monasteries in France and in Rome, believed unquestioningly in the value of prayers of intercession for the success of the apostolic work. Only in Heaven will we understand how much the prayer of cloistered religious effectively accompanies apostolic action! To each and every one of them I address my grateful and affectionate thoughts.

Dear brothers and sisters, may the life of Dominic de Guzmán spur us all to be fervent in prayer, courageous in living out our faith, and deeply in love with Jesus Christ. Through his intercession, let us ask God always to enrich the Church with authentic preachers of the Gospel.

4

Saint Anthony of Padua

WEDNESDAY, 10 FEBRUARY 2010
Paul VI Audience Hall

Dear Brothers and Sisters,

Two weeks ago I presented Saint Francis of Assisi. This morning I would like to speak of another saint who belonged to the first generation of the Friars Minor: Anthony of Padua, or of Lisbon, as he is also called with reference to his native town. He is one of the most popular saints in the whole Catholic Church, venerated not only in Padua, where a splendid Basilica has been built that contains his mortal remains, but also throughout the world. Dear to the faithful are the images and statues that portray him with the lily—a symbol of his purity—or with the Child Jesus in his arms, in memory of a miraculous apparition mentioned in several literary sources.

With his outstanding gifts of intelligence, balance, apostolic zeal, and, primarily, mystic fervor, Anthony contributed significantly to the development of Franciscan spirituality.

He was born into a noble family in Lisbon in about 1195 and was baptized with the name of Fernando. He entered the Canons who followed the monastic Rule of Saint Augustine, first at Saint Vincent's Monastery in Lisbon and later at that of the Holy Cross in Coimbra, a renowned cultural center in Portugal. He dedicated himself with interest and solicitude to the study of the Bible and of the Church Fathers, acquiring the theological knowledge that was to bear fruit in his teaching and preaching activities. The event that represented a decisive turning point in his life happened in Coimbra. It was there, in 1220, that the relics were exposed of the first five Franciscan missionaries who had gone to Morocco, where they had met with martyrdom. Their story inspired in young Fernando the desire to imitate them and to advance on the path of Christian perfection. Thus he asked to leave the Augustinian Canons to become a Friar Minor. His request was granted, and, having taken the name of Anthony, he too set out for Morocco, but divine Providence disposed otherwise. After an illness he was obliged to return to Italy and, in 1221, he participated in the famous "Chapter of the Mats" in Assisi, where he also met Saint Francis. He then lived for a period in complete seclusion in a convent at Forlì in northern Italy, where the Lord called him to another mission. Invited, in somewhat casual circumstances, to preach on the occasion of a priestly ordination, he showed himself to be endowed with such knowledge and eloquence that the Superiors assigned him to preaching. Thus he embarked on apostolic work in Italy and France that was so intense and effective that it induced many people who had left the Church to retrace their footsteps. Anthony was also one of the first, if not the first, theology teachers of the Friars Minor. He began his teaching in Bologna with the blessing of Saint Francis, who, recognizing Anthony's virtues, sent him a short letter that began with these words: "I would like you to teach the brethren theology." Anthony laid the foundations of Franciscan theology which, cultivated by other outstanding thinkers, was to reach its apex with Saint Bonaventure of Bagnoregio and Blessed Duns Scotus.

Having become Provincial Superior of the Friars Minor in northern Italy, he continued his ministry of preaching, alternating it with his office of governance. When his term as Provincial came to an end, he withdrew to a place near Padua where he had stayed on various other occasions. Barely a year later, he died at the city gates on 13 June 1231. Padua, which had welcomed him with affection and veneration in his lifetime, has always accorded him honor and devotion. Pope Gregory IX himself, having heard him preach, described him as the "Ark of the Testament" and, subsequent to miracles brought about through his intercession, canonized him in 1232, only a year after his death.

In the last period of his life, Anthony put in writing two cycles of "Sermons", entitled respectively "Sunday Sermons" and "Sermons on the Saints", destined for the Franciscan Order's preachers and teachers of theological studies. In these sermons he commented on the texts of Scripture presented by the Liturgy, using the patristic and medieval interpretation of the four senses: the literal or historical, the allegorical or Christological, the tropological or moral, and the anagogical, which orients a person to eternal life. Today it has been rediscovered that these senses are dimensions of the one meaning of Sacred Scripture and that it is right to interpret Sacred Scripture by seeking the four dimensions of its words. Saint Anthony's sermons are theological and homiletical texts that echo the live preaching in which Anthony proposes a true and proper itinerary of Christian life. The richness of spiritual teaching contained in the "Sermons" was so great that in 1946 Venerable Pope Pius XII proclaimed Anthony a Doctor of the Church, attributing to him the title "Doctor Evangelicus", since the freshness and beauty of the Gospel emerge from these writings. We can still read them today with great spiritual profit.

In these sermons, Saint Anthony speaks of prayer as of a loving relationship that impels man to speak gently with the Lord, creating an ineffable joy that sweetly enfolds the soul in prayer. Anthony reminds us that prayer requires an atmosphere of silence, which does not mean distance from external noise but, rather, is an interior experience that aims to remove the distractions caused by a soul's anxieties, thereby creating silence in the soul itself. According to this prominent Franciscan Doctor's teaching, prayer is structured in four indispensable attitudes, which in Anthony's Latin are defined as *obsecratio, oratio, postulatio, gratiarum actio*. We might translate them in the following manner. The first step in prayer is confidently opening one's heart to God; this is not merely accepting a word but opening one's heart to God's presence. Next is speaking with him affectionately, seeing him present with oneself; then—a very natural thing—presenting our needs to him; and lastly, praising and thanking him.

In Saint Anthony's teaching on prayer, we perceive one of the specific traits of the Franciscan theology that he founded: namely, the role assigned to divine love, which enters into the sphere of the affections, of the will, and of the heart and which is also the source from which flows a spiritual knowledge that surpasses all other knowledge. In fact, it is in loving that we come to know.

Anthony writes further: "Charity is the soul of faith; it gives it life; without love, faith dies" (*Sermones Dominicales et Festivi* II, Messagero, Padua, 1979, p. 37).

It is only the prayerful soul that can progress in spiritual life: this is the privileged object of Saint Anthony's preaching. He is thoroughly familiar with the shortcomings of human nature, with our tendency to lapse into sin, which is why he continuously urges us to fight the inclination to avidity, pride, and impurity and to practice instead the virtues of poverty and generosity, of humility and obedience, of chastity and of purity. At the beginning of the thirteenth century, in the context of the rebirth of the city and the flourishing of trade, the number of people who were insensitive to the needs of the poor increased. This is why on various occasions Anthony invites the faithful to think of the true riches, those of the heart, which make people good and merciful and permit them to lay up treasure in Heaven. "O rich people", he urged them, "befriend . . . the poor, welcome them into your homes: it will subsequently be they who receive you in the eternal tabernacles in which is the beauty of peace, the confidence of security, and the opulent tranquility of eternal satiety" (*ibid.*, p. 29).

Is not this, dear friends, perhaps a very important teaching today, too, when the financial crisis and serious economic inequalities impoverish many people and create conditions of poverty? In my Encyclical *Caritas in Veritate* I recall: "The economy needs ethics in order to function correctly—not any ethics whatsoever, but an ethics which is people-centered" (no. 45).

Anthony, in the school of Francis, always put Christ at the center of his life and thinking, of his action, and of his preaching. This is another characteristic feature of Franciscan theology: Christocentrism. Franciscan theology willingly contemplates and invites others to contemplate the mysteries of the Lord's humanity, the man Jesus, and in a special way the mystery of the Nativity: God who made himself a Child and gave himself into our hands, a mystery that gives rise to sentiments of love and gratitude for divine goodness.

Not only the Nativity, a central point of Christ's love for humanity, but also the vision of the Crucified One inspired in Anthony thoughts of gratitude to God and esteem for the dignity of the human person, so that all believers and non-believers might find in the Crucified One and in his image a life-enriching meaning. Saint Anthony writes: "Christ who is your life is hanging before you, so that you may look at the Cross as in a mirror. There you will be able to know how mortal were your wounds, which no medicine other than the Blood of the Son of God could heal. If you look closely, you will be able to realize how great your human dignity and your value are. . . . Nowhere other than looking at himself in the mirror of the Cross can man better understand how much he is worth" (*Sermones Dominicales et Festivi* III, pp. 213–14).

In meditating on these words, we are better able to understand the importance of the image of the Crucified One for our culture, for our humanity that is born from the Christian faith. Precisely by looking at the Crucified One, we see, as Saint Anthony says, how great are the dignity and worth of man. At no other point can we understand how much man is worth, precisely because God makes us so important, considers us so important that, in his opinion, we are worthy of his suffering; thus all human dignity appears in the mirror of the Crucified One, and our gazing upon him is ever a source of acknowledgment of human dignity.

Dear friends, may Anthony of Padua, so widely venerated by the faithful, intercede for the whole Church and especially for those who are dedicated to preaching; let us pray the Lord that he will help us learn a little of this art from Saint Anthony. May preachers, drawing inspiration from his example, be effective in their communication by taking pains to combine solid and sound doctrine with sincere and fervent devotion. In this Year for Priests, let us pray that priests and deacons will carry out with concern this ministry of the proclamation of the word of God, making it timely for the faithful, especially through liturgical homilies. May they effectively present the eternal beauty of Christ, just as Anthony recommended: "If you preach Jesus, he will melt hardened hearts; if you invoke him, he will soften harsh temptations; if you think of him, he will enlighten your mind; if you read of him, he will satisfy your intellect" (*Sermones Dominicales et Festivi* III, p. 59).

5

Saint Bonaventure (1)

WEDNESDAY, 3 MARCH 2010

Paul VI Audience Hall

Dear Brothers and Sisters,

Today I would like to talk about Saint Bonaventure of Bagnoregio. I confide to you that in broaching this subject I feel a certain nostalgia, for I am thinking back to my research as a young scholar on this author who was particularly dear to me. My knowledge of him had quite an impact on my formation. A few months ago, with great joy, I made a pilgrimage to the place of his birth, Bagnoregio, an Italian town in Lazio that venerates his memory.

Saint Bonaventure, in all likelihood born in 1217, died in 1274. Thus he lived in the thirteenth century, an epoch in which the Christian faith—which had deeply penetrated the culture and society of Europe—inspired imperishable works in the fields of literature, the visual arts, philosophy, and theology. Among the great Christian figures who contributed to the composition of this harmony between faith and culture Bonaventure stands out, a man of action and contemplation, of profound piety and prudent government.

He was called Giovanni di Fidanza. An episode that occurred when he was still a boy deeply marked his life, as he himself recounts. He fell seriously ill, and even his father, who was a doctor, gave up all hope of saving him from death. So his mother had recourse to the intercession of Saint Francis of Assisi, who had recently been canonized. And Giovanni recovered.

The figure of the *Poverello* of Assisi became even more familiar to him several years later when he was in Paris, where he had gone to pursue his studies. He had obtained a Master of Arts Diploma, which we could compare with that of a prestigious secondary school in our time. At that point, like so many young men in the past and also today, Giovanni asked himself a crucial question: "What should I do with my life?" Fascinated by the witness of fervor and evangelical radicalism of the Friars Minor who had arrived in Paris in 1219, Giovanni knocked at the door of the Franciscan convent in that city and asked to be admitted to the great family of Saint Francis' disciples. Many years later he explained the reasons for his decision: he recognized Christ's action in Saint Francis and in the movement he had founded. Thus he wrote in a letter addressed to another friar: "I confess before God that the reason which made me love the life of blessed Francis most is that it resembled the birth and early development of the Church. The Church began with simple fishermen and was subsequently enriched by very distinguished and wise teachers; the religion of Blessed Francis was established, not by the prudence of men, but by Christ" (*Epistula de tribus quaestionibus ad magistrum innominatum*, in *Opere di San Bonaventura: Introduzione generale*, Rome, 1990, p. 29).

So it was that in about the year 1243 Giovanni was clothed in the Franciscan habit and took the name "Bonaventure". He was immediately sent to study and attended the Faculty of Theology of the University of Paris, where he took a series of very demanding courses. He obtained the various qualifications required for an academic career, earning a bachelor's degree in Scripture and in the *Sentences*. Thus Bonaventure studied profoundly Sacred Scripture, the *Sentences* of Peter Lombard—the theology manual in that time—and the most important theological authors. He was in contact with the teachers and students from across Europe who converged in Paris, and he developed his own personal thinking and a spiritual sensitivity of great value with which, in the following years, he was able to infuse his works and his sermons, thus becoming one of the most important theologians in the history of the Church. It is important to remember the title of the thesis he defended in order to qualify to teach theology, the *licentia ubique docendi*, as it was then called. His dissertation was entitled *Questions on the Knowledge of Christ*. This subject reveals the central role that Christ always played in Bonaventure's life and teaching. We may certainly say that the whole of his thinking was profoundly Christocentric.

In those years in Paris, Bonaventure's adopted city, a violent dispute was raging against the Friars Minor of Saint Francis Assisi and the Friars Preachers of Saint Dominic de Guzmán. Their right to teach at the university was contested, and doubt was even being cast upon the authenticity of their consecrated life. Of course, the changes introduced by the Mendicant Orders in the way of understanding religious life, of which I have spoken in previous Catecheses, were so entirely new that not everyone managed to understand them. Then it should be added, just as sometimes happens even among sincerely religious people, that human weakness, such as envy and jealousy, came into play. Although Bonaventure was confronted by the opposition of the other university masters, he had already begun to teach at the Franciscans' Chair of theology, and, to respond to those who were challenging the Mendicant Orders, he composed a text entitled *Evangelical Perfection*. In this work he shows how the Mendicant Orders, especially the Friars Minor, in practicing the vows of poverty, chastity, and obedience, were following the recommendations of the Gospel itself. Over and above these historical circumstances, the teaching that Bonaventure provides in this work of his and in his life remains ever timely: the Church is made more luminous and beautiful by the fidelity to their vocation of those sons and daughters of hers who not only put the evangelical precepts into practice but, by the grace of God, are called to observe their counsels and thereby, with their poor, chaste, and obedient way of life, to witness to the Gospel as a source of joy and perfection.

The storm blew over, at least for a while, and through the personal intervention of Pope Alexander VI in 1257, Bonaventure was officially recognized as a doctor and master of the University of Paris. However, he was obliged to relinquish this prestigious office because in that same year the General Chapter of the Order elected him Minister General.

He fulfilled this office for seventeen years with wisdom and dedication, visiting the provinces, writing to his brethren, and at times intervening with some severity to eliminate abuses. When Bonaventure began this service, the Order of Friars Minor had experienced an extraordinary expansion: there were more than 30,000 friars scattered throughout the West with missionaries in North Africa, the Middle East, and even in Peking. It was necessary to consolidate this expansion and, especially, to give it unity of action and of spirit in full fidelity to Francis' charism. In fact, different ways of interpreting the message of the Saint of Assisi arose among his followers, and they ran a real risk of an internal split. To avoid this danger, in 1260 the General Chapter of the Order in Narbonne accepted and ratified a text proposed by Bonaventure in which the norms regulating the daily life of the Friars Minor were collected and unified. Bonaventure, however, foresaw that, regardless of the wisdom and moderation which inspired the legislative measures, they would not suffice to guarantee communion of spirit and hearts. It was necessary to share the same ideals and the same motivations.

For this reason, Bonaventure wished to present the authentic charism of Francis, his life, and his teaching. Thus he zealously collected documents concerning the *Poverello* and listened attentively to the memories of those who had actually known Francis. This inspired a historically well-founded biography of the Saint of Assisi, entitled *Legenda Maior*. It was redrafted more concisely, hence entitled *Legenda minor*. Unlike the Italian term, the Latin word does not mean a product of the imagination, but, on the contrary, "*Legenda*" means an authoritative text, "to be read" officially. Indeed, the General Chapter of the Friars Minor in 1263, meeting in Pisa, recognized Saint Bonaventure's biography as the most faithful portrait of their Founder, and so it became the Saint's official biography.

What image of Saint Francis emerged from the heart and pen of his follower and successor Saint Bonaventure? The key point: Francis is an *alter Christus*, a man who sought Christ passionately. In the love that impelled Francis to imitate Christ, he was entirely conformed to Christ. Bonaventure pointed out this living ideal to all Francis' followers. This ideal, valid for every Christian, yesterday, today, and forever, was also proposed as a program for the Church in the Third Millennium by my Predecessor, Venerable John Paul II. This program, he wrote in his Letter *Novo Millennio Ineunte*, is centered "in Christ himself, who is to be known, loved, and imitated, so that in him we may live the life of the Trinity and, with him, transform history until its fulfillment in the heavenly Jerusalem" (no. 29).

In 1273, Saint Bonaventure experienced another great change in his life. Pope Gregory X wanted to consecrate him a Bishop and to appoint him a Cardinal. The Pope also asked him to prepare the Second Ecumenical Council of Lyons, a most important ecclesial event, for the purpose of re-establishing communion between the Latin Church and the Greek Church. He dedicated himself diligently to this task but was unable to see the conclusion of this ecumenical session because he died before it ended. An anonymous papal notary composed a eulogy to Bonaventure which gives us a conclusive portrait of this great Saint and excellent theologian. "A good, affable, devout, and compassionate man, full of virtue, beloved of God and human beings alike.... God in fact had bestowed upon him such grace that all who saw him were pervaded by a love that their hearts could not conceal" (cf. J. G. Bougerol, *Bonaventura*, in A. Vauchez [ed.], *Storia dei santi e della santità cristiana*. Vol. VI. *L'epoca del rinnovamento evangelico*, Milan, 1991, p. 91).

Let us gather the heritage of this holy Doctor of the Church, who reminds us of the meaning of our life with the following words: "On earth ... we may contemplate the divine immensity through reasoning and admiration; in the heavenly homeland, on the other hand, through the vision, when we are likened to God, and through ecstasy ... we shall enter into the joy of God" (*La conoscenza di Cristo, q. 6, conclusione*, in *Opere di San Bonaventura: Opuscoli Teologici*/1, Rome, 1993, p. 187).

6

Saint Bonaventure (2)

WEDNESDAY, 10 MARCH 2010
Paul VI Audience Hall

Dear Brothers and Sisters,

Last week I spoke of the life and personality of Saint Bonaventure of Bagnoregio. This morning I would like to continue my presentation, reflecting on part of his literary opus and on his doctrine.

As I have already said, among Saint Bonaventure's various merits was the ability to interpret authentically and faithfully Saint Francis of Assisi, whom he venerated and studied with deep love.

In a special way, in Saint Bonaventure's day a movement among the Friars Minor known as the "Spirituals" held that Saint Francis had ushered in a totally new phase in history and that the "eternal Gospel", of which revelation speaks, had come to replace the New Testament. This group declared that the Church had now fulfilled her role in history. They said that she had been replaced by a charismatic community of free men guided from within by the Spirit, namely, the "Spiritual Franciscans". This group's ideas were based on the writings of a Cistercian abbot, Joachim of Fiore, who died in 1202. In his works he affirmed a Trinitarian rhythm in history. He considered the Old

Testament as the age of the Fathers, followed by the time of the Son, the time of the Church. The third age was to be awaited, that of the Holy Spirit. The whole of history was thus interpreted as a history of progress: from the severity of the Old Testament to the relative freedom of the time of the Son, in the Church, to the full freedom of the Sons of God in the period of the Holy Spirit. This, finally, was also to be the period of peace among mankind, of the reconciliation of peoples and of religions. Joachim of Fiore had awakened the hope that the new age would stem from a new form of monasticism. Thus it is understandable that a group of Franciscans might have thought it recognized Saint Francis of Assisi as the initiator of the new epoch and his Order as the community of the new period—the community of the Age of the Holy Spirit that left behind the hierarchical Church in order to begin the new Church of the Spirit, no longer linked to the old structures.

Hence they ran the risk of very seriously misunderstanding Saint Francis' message, of his humble fidelity to the Gospel and to the Church. This error entailed an erroneous vision of Christianity as a whole.

Saint Bonaventure, who became Minister General of the Franciscan Order in 1257, had to confront grave tension in his Order precisely because of those who supported the above-mentioned movement of the "Franciscan Spirituals" who followed Joachim of Fiore. To respond to this group and to restore unity to the Order, Saint Bonaventure painstakingly studied the authentic writings of Joachim of Fiore, as well as those attributed to him, and, bearing in mind the need to present the figure and message of his beloved Saint Francis correctly, he wanted to set down a correct view of the theology of history. Saint Bonaventure actually tackled the problem in his last work, a collection of conferences for the monks of the *studium* in Paris. He did not complete it, and it has come down to us through the transcriptions of those who heard him. It is entitled *Hexaëmeron*, in other words, an allegorical explanation of the six days of creation. The Fathers of the Church considered the six or seven days of the creation narrative as a prophecy of the history of the world, of mankind. For them, the seven days represented seven periods of history, later also interpreted as seven millennia. With Christ we should have entered the last, that is, the sixth period of history that was to be followed by the great sabbath of God. Saint Bonaventure hypothesizes this historical interpretation of the account of the days of creation, but in a very free and innovative way. To his mind, two phenomena of his time required a new interpretation of the course of history.

The first: the figure of Saint Francis, the man totally united with Christ even to communion with the stigmata, almost an *alter Christus*, and, with Saint Francis, the new community he created, different from the monasticism known until then. This phenomenon called for a new interpretation, as an innovation of God which appeared at that moment.

The second: the position of Joachim of Fiore, who announced a new monasticism and a totally new period of history, going beyond the revelation of the New Testament, demanded a response. As Minister General of the Franciscan Order, Saint Bonaventure had immediately realized that with the spiritualistic conception inspired by Joachim of Fiore, the Order would become ungovernable and logically move toward anarchy. In his opinion, this had two consequences:

The first, the practical need for structures and for insertion into the reality of the hierarchical Church, of the real Church, required a theological foundation. This was partly because the others, those who followed the spiritualist concept, upheld what seemed to have a theological foundation.

The second, while taking into account the necessary realism, made it essential not to lose the newness of the figure of Saint Francis.

How did Saint Bonaventure respond to the practical and theoretical needs? Here I can provide only a very basic summary of his answer, and it is in certain aspects incomplete:

1. Saint Bonaventure rejected the idea of the Trinitarian rhythm of history. God is one for all history and is not tritheistic. Hence history is one, even if it is a journey and, according to Saint Bonaventure, a journey of progress.

2. Jesus Christ is God's last word—in him God said all, giving and expressing himself. More than himself, God cannot express or give. The Holy Spirit is the Spirit of the Father and of the Son. Christ himself says of the Holy Spirit: "He will bring to your remembrance all that I have said to you" (Jn 14:26), and "he will take what is mine and declare it to you" (Jn 16:15). Thus there is no loftier Gospel, there is no other Church to await. Therefore the Order of Saint Francis, too, must fit into this Church, into her faith and into her hierarchical order.

3. This does not mean that the Church is stationary, fixed in the past, or that there can be no newness within her. "*Opera Christi non deficiunt, sed proficiunt*": Christ's works do not go backward, they do not fail but progress, the Saint said in his letter *De Tribus Quaestionibus*. Thus Saint Bonaventure explicitly formulates the idea of progress, and this is an innovation in comparison with the Fathers of the Church and the majority of his contemporaries. For Saint Bonaventure, Christ was no longer the end of history, as he was for the Fathers of the Church, but rather its center; history does not end with Christ but begins a new period. The

following is another consequence: until that moment the idea that the Fathers of the Church were the absolute summit of theology predominated; all successive generations could only be their disciples. Saint Bonaventure also recognized the Fathers as teachers forever, but the phenomenon of Saint Francis assured him that the riches of Christ's word are inexhaustible and that new light could also appear to the new generations. The oneness of Christ also guarantees newness and renewal in all the periods of history.

The Franciscan Order, of course—as he emphasized—belongs to the Church of Jesus Christ, to the apostolic Church, and cannot be built on utopian spiritualism. Yet, at the same time, the newness of this Order in comparison with classical monasticism was valid, and Saint Bonaventure—as I said in my previous Catechesis—defended this newness against the attacks of the secular clergy of Paris: the Franciscans have no fixed monastery; they may go everywhere to proclaim the Gospel. It was precisely the break with stability, the characteristic of monasticism, for the sake of a new flexibility that restored to the Church her missionary dynamism.

At this point it might be useful to say that today, too, there are views that see the entire history of the Church in the second millennium as a gradual decline. Some see this decline as having already begun immediately after the New Testament. In fact, "*Opera Christi non deficiunt, sed proficiunt*": Christ's works do not go backward but forward. What would the Church be without the new spirituality of the Cistercians, the Franciscans, and the Dominicans, the spirituality of Saint Teresa of Avila and Saint John of the Cross, and so forth? This affirmation applies today too: "*Opera Christi non deficiunt, sed proficiunt*", they move forward. Saint Bonaventure teaches us the need for overall, even strict discernment, sober realism, and openness to the newness, which

Christ gives his Church through the Holy Spirit. And while this idea of decline is repeated, another idea, this "spiritualistic utopianism", is also reiterated. Indeed, we know that after the Second Vatican Council some were convinced that everything was new, that there was a different Church, that the pre-Conciliar Church was finished, and that we had another, totally "other" Church. An anarchic utopianism! And thanks be to God the wise helmsmen of the Barque of Saint Peter, Pope Paul VI, and Pope John Paul II, on the one hand, defended the newness of the Council and, on the other, defended the oneness and continuity of the Church, which is always a Church of sinners and always a place of grace.

4. In this regard, Saint Bonaventure, as Minister General of the Franciscans, took a line of government which showed clearly that the new Order could not, as a community, live at the same "eschatological height" as Saint Francis, in whom he saw the future world anticipated, but, guided at the same time by healthy realism and by spiritual courage, he had to come as close as possible to the maximum realization of the Sermon on the Mount, which for Saint Francis was *the* rule, but nevertheless bearing in mind the limitations of the human being who is marked by original sin.

Thus we see that for Saint Bonaventure governing was not merely action but, above all, was thinking and praying. At the root of his government we always find prayer and thought; all his decisions are the result of reflection, of thought illumined by prayer. His intimate contact with Christ always accompanied his work as Minister General, and therefore he composed a series of theological and mystical writings that express the soul of his government. They also manifest his intention of guiding the Order inwardly, that is, of governing not only by means of commands and structures, but by guiding and illuminating souls, orienting them to Christ.

I would like to mention only one of these writings, which are the soul of his government and point out the way to follow, both for the individual and for the community: the *Itinerarium mentis in Deum* [*The Journey of the Mind into God*], which is a "manual" for mystical contemplation. This book was conceived in a deeply spiritual place: Mount La Verna, where Saint Francis had received the stigmata. In the introduction the author describes the circumstances that gave rise to this writing: "While I meditated on the possible ascent of the mind to God, among other things there occurred that miracle which happened in the same place to the blessed Francis himself, namely, the vision of the winged Seraph in the form of a Crucifix. While meditating upon this vision, I immediately saw that it offered me the ecstatic contemplation of Father Francis himself as well as the way that leads to it" (cf. *The Journey of the Mind into God*, Prologue, 2, in *Opere di San Bonaventura. Opuscoli Teologici*/1, Rome, 1993, p. 499).

The six wings of the Seraph thus became the symbol of the six stages that lead man progressively from the knowledge of God, through the observation of the world and creatures and through the exploration of the soul itself with its faculties, to the satisfying union with the Trinity through Christ, in imitation of Saint Francis of Assisi. The last words of Saint Bonaventure's *Itinerarium*, which respond to the question of how it is possible to reach this mystical communion with God, should be made to sink to the depths of the heart:

> If you should wish to know how these things come about (the mystical communion with God), question grace, not instruction; desire, not intellect; the cry of prayer, not pursuit of study; the spouse, not the teacher; God, not man; darkness, not clarity; not light, but the fire that inflames all

> and transports to God with fullest unction and burning affection. . . . Let us then . . . pass over into darkness; let us impose silence on cares, concupiscence, and phantasms; let us pass over *with the Crucified Christ from this world to the Father*, so that when the Father is shown to us we may say with Philip, "*It is enough for me*". (Cf. *ibid.*, VII, 6)

Dear friends, let us accept the invitation addressed to us by Saint Bonaventure, the Seraphic Doctor, and learn at the school of the divine Teacher: let us listen to his word of life and truth that resonates in the depths of our soul. Let us purify our thoughts and actions so that he may dwell within us and that we may understand his divine voice, which draws us toward true happiness.

7

Saint Bonaventure (3)

WEDNESDAY, 17 MARCH 2010

Paul VI Audience Hall

Dear Brothers and Sisters,

This morning, continuing last Wednesday's reflection, I would like to study with you some other aspects of the doctrine of Saint Bonaventure of Bagnoregio. He is an eminent theologian who deserves to be set beside another great thinker, a contemporary of his, Saint Thomas Aquinas. Both scrutinized the mysteries of revelation, making the most of the resources of human reason, in the fruitful dialogue between faith and reason that characterized the Christian Middle Ages, making it a time of great intellectual vigor as well as of faith and ecclesial renewal, which is often not sufficiently emphasized. Other similarities link them: Both Bonaventure, a Franciscan, and Thomas, a Dominican, belonged to the Mendicant Orders, which, with their spiritual freshness, as I mentioned in previous Catecheses, renewed the whole Church in the thirteenth century and attracted many followers. They both served the Church with diligence, passion, and love, to the point that they were invited to take part in the Ecumenical Council of Lyons in 1274, the very same year in which they died; Thomas while he was on his way to Lyons, Bonaventure while the Council was taking place.

Even the statues of the two Saints in Saint Peter's Square are parallel. They stand right at the beginning of the colonnade, starting from the façade of the Vatican Basilica; one is on the left wing, and the other on the right. Despite all these aspects, in these two great Saints we can discern two different approaches to philosophical and theological research which show the originality and depth of the thinking of each. I would like to point out some of their differences.

A first difference concerns the concept of theology. Both Doctors wondered whether theology was a practical or a theoretical and speculative science. Saint Thomas reflects on two possible contrasting answers. The first says: theology is a reflection on faith, and the purpose of faith is that man become good and live in accordance with God's will. Hence the aim of theology would be to guide people on the right, good road; thus it is basically a practical science. The other position says: theology seeks to know God. We are the work of God; God is above our action. God works right action in us; so it essentially concerns, not our own doing, but knowing God, not our own actions. Saint Thomas' conclusion is: theology entails both aspects: it is theoretical, it seeks to know God ever better, and it is practical: it seeks to orient our life to the good. But there is a primacy of knowledge: above all we must know God and, then, continue to act in accordance with God (*Summa Theologiae*, Ia, q. 1, art. 4). This primacy of knowledge in comparison with practice is significant for Saint Thomas' fundamental orientation.

Saint Bonaventure's answer is very similar, but the stress he gives is different. Saint Bonaventure knows the same arguments for both directions, as does Saint Thomas, but in answer to the question as to whether theology is a practical or a theoretical science, Saint Bonaventure makes a triple distinction—he therefore extends the alternative between the theoretical (the primacy of knowledge) and the practical (the primacy of practice), adding a third attitude which he calls "sapiential" and affirming that wisdom embraces both aspects. And he continues: wisdom seeks contemplation (as the highest form of knowledge) and has as its intention "*ut boni fiamus*"—that we become good, especially this: to become good (cf. *Breviloquium*, *Prologus*, 5). He then adds: "Faith is in the intellect, in such a way that it provokes affection. For example: the knowledge that Christ died 'for us' does not remain knowledge but necessarily becomes affection, love" (*Proemium in I Sent.*, q. 3).

His defense of theology is along the same lines, namely, of the rational and methodical reflection on faith. Saint Bonaventure lists several arguments against engaging in theology perhaps also widespread among a section of the Franciscan friars and also present in our time: that reason would empty faith, that it would be an aggressive attitude to the word of God, that we should listen and not analyze the word of God (cf. *Letter of Saint Francis of Assisi to Saint Anthony of Padua*). The Saint responds to these arguments against theology that demonstrate the perils that exist in theology itself, saying: it is true that there is an arrogant manner of engaging in theology, a pride of reason that sets itself above the word of God. Yet real theology, the rational work of the true and good theology, has another origin, not the pride of reason. One who loves wants to know his beloved better and better; true theology does not involve reason and its research prompted by pride, "*sed propter amorem eius cui assentit*—[but is] motivated by love of the One who gave his consent" (*Proemium in I Sent.*, q. 2) and wants to be better acquainted with the beloved: this is the fundamental intention of theology. Thus in the end, for Saint Bonaventure, the primacy of love is crucial.

Consequently Saint Thomas and Saint Bonaventure define man's final goal, his complete happiness, in different ways. For Saint Thomas, the supreme end, to which our desire is directed, is: to see God. In this simple act of seeing God all problems are solved: we are happy; nothing else is necessary.

Instead, for Saint Bonaventure the ultimate destiny of man is to love God, to encounter him, and to be united in his and our love. For him, this is the most satisfactory definition of our happiness.

Along these lines we could also say that the loftiest category for Saint Thomas is the true, whereas for Saint Bonaventure it is the good. It would be mistaken to see a contradiction in these two answers. For both of them, the true is also the good, and the good is also the true; to see God is to love, and to love is to see. Hence it was a question of their different interpretation of a fundamentally shared vision. Both emphases have given shape to different traditions and different spiritualities and have thus shown the fruitfulness of the faith: one, in the diversity of its expressions.

Let us return to Saint Bonaventure. It is obvious that the specific emphasis he gave to his theology, of which I have given only one example, is explained on the basis of the Franciscan charism. The *Poverello* of Assisi, notwithstanding the intellectual debates of his time, had shown with his whole life the primacy of love. He was a living icon of Christ in love with Christ, and thus he made the figure of the Lord present in his time—he convinced his contemporaries, not with his words, but rather with his life. In all Saint Bonaventure's works, precisely also his scientific works, his scholarly works, one sees and finds this Franciscan inspiration; in other words, one notices that his thought starts with his encounter with the *Poverello* of Assisi. However, in order to understand the practical elaboration of the topic "primacy of love", we must bear in mind yet another source: the writings of the so-called Pseudo-Dionysius, a Syrian theologian of the sixth century who concealed himself behind the pseudonym of Dionysius the Areopagite. In the choice of this name, he was referring to a figure in the Acts of the Apostles (cf. 17:34). This theologian had created a liturgical theology and a mystical theology and had spoken extensively of the different orders of angels. His writings were translated into Latin in the ninth century. At the time of Saint Bonaventure—we are in the thirteenth century—a new tradition appeared that aroused the interest of the Saint and of other theologians of his century. Two things in particular attracted Saint Bonaventure's attention.

1. Pseudo-Dionysius speaks of nine orders of angels whose names he had found in Scripture and then organized in his own way, from the simple angels to the seraphim. Saint Bonaventure interprets these orders of angels as steps on the human creature's way to God. Thus they can represent the human journey, the ascent toward communion with God. For Saint Bonaventure, there is no doubt: Saint Francis of Assisi belonged to the Seraphic Order, to the supreme Order, to the choir of seraphim, namely, he was a pure flame of love. And this is what Franciscans should have been. But Saint Bonaventure knew well that this final step in the approach to God could not be inserted into a juridical order but is always a special gift of God. For this reason, the structure of the Franciscan Order is more modest, more realistic, but nevertheless must help its members to come ever closer to a seraphic existence of pure love. Last Wednesday I spoke of this synthesis between sober realism and evangelical radicalism in the thought and action of Saint Bonaventure.

2. Saint Bonaventure, however, found in the writings of Peusdo-Dionysius another element, an even more important

one. Whereas for Saint Augustine the *intellectus*, the seeing with reason and the heart, is the ultimate category of knowledge, Pseudo-Dionysius takes a further step: in the ascent toward God one can reach a point in which reason no longer sees. But in the night of the intellect, love still sees it—sees what is inaccessible to reason. Love goes beyond reason, it sees farther, it enters more profoundly into God's mystery. Saint Bonaventure was fascinated by this vision, which converged with his own Franciscan spirituality. It is precisely in the dark night of the Cross that divine love appears in its full grandeur; where reason no longer sees, love sees. The final words of his *The Journey of the Mind into God* can seem to a superficial interpretation an exaggerated expression of devotion devoid of content; instead, read in the light of Saint Bonaventure's theology of the Cross, they are a clear and realistic expression of Franciscan spirituality: "If you should wish to know how these things come about (the mystical communion with God), question grace, not instruction, desire, not intellect; the cry of prayer, not pursuit of study . . . not light, but the fire that inflames all and transports to God" (VII, 6). All this is neither anti-intellectual nor anti-rational: it implies the process of reason, but transcends it in the love of the Crucified Christ. With this transformation of the mysticism of Pseudo-Dionysius, Saint Bonaventure is placed at the source of a great mystical current which has greatly raised and purified the human mind: it is a lofty peak in the history of the human spirit.

This theology of the Cross, born of the encounter of Pseudo-Dionysius' theology and Franciscan spirituality, must not make us forget that Saint Bonaventure also shares with Saint Francis of Assisi his love for creation, his joy at the beauty of God's creation. On this point I cite a sentence from the first chapter of the *Journey*: "He who is not brightened by such splendors of created things is blind; he who does not awake at such clamors is deaf; he who does not praise God on account of all these effects is mute; he who does not turn toward the First Principle on account of such indications is stupid" (I, 15).

The whole creation speaks loudly of God, of the good and beautiful God; of his love. Hence for Saint Bonaventure the whole of our life is a "journey", a pilgrimage, an ascent to God. But with our own strength alone, we are incapable of climbing to the loftiness of God. God himself must help us, must "pull" us up. Thus prayer is necessary. Prayer, says the Saint, is the mother and the origin of the upward movement—"*sursum actio*", an action that lifts us up, Bonaventure says. Accordingly I conclude with the prayer with which he begins his *Journey*: "Let us therefore say to the Lord our God: 'Lead me forth, Lord, in thy way, and let me step in thy truth; let my heart be glad, that it fears thy name'" (I, 1).

8

Saint Albert the Great

WEDNESDAY, 24 MARCH 2010

Saint Peter's Square

Dear Brothers and Sisters,

One of the great masters of medieval theology is Saint Albert the Great. The title "Great" (*Magnus*) with which he has passed into history indicates the vastness and depth of his teaching, which he combined with holiness of life. However, his contemporaries did not hesitate to attribute to him titles of excellence even then. One of his disciples, Ulric of Strasbourg, called him the "wonder and miracle of our epoch".

He was born in Germany at the beginning of the thirteenth century. When he was still young he went to Italy, to Padua, the seat of one of the most famous medieval universities. He devoted himself to the study of the so-called "liberal arts": grammar, rhetoric, dialectics, arithmetic, geometry, astronomy, and music, that is, to culture in general, demonstrating that characteristic interest in the natural sciences which was soon to become the favorite field for his specialization. During his stay in Padua, he attended the Church of the Dominicans, whom he then joined with the profession of the religious vows. Hagiographic sources suggest that Albert came to this decision gradually. His intense relationship with God, the Dominican friars' example of holiness, hearing the sermons of Blessed Jordan of Saxony, Saint Dominic's successor as the Master General of the Order of Preachers, were the decisive factors that helped him to overcome every doubt and even to surmount his family's resistance. God often speaks to us in the years of our youth and points out to us the project of our life. As it was for Albert, so also for all of us, personal prayer, nourished by the Lord's word, frequent reception of the sacraments, and the spiritual guidance of enlightened people are the means to discover and follow God's voice. He received the religious habit from Blessed Jordan of Saxony.

After his ordination to the priesthood, his superiors sent him to teach at various theological study centers annexed to the convents of the Dominican Fathers. His brilliant intellectual qualities enabled him to perfect his theological studies at the most famous university in that period, the University of Paris. From that time on, Saint Albert began his extraordinary activity as a writer, which he was to pursue throughout his life.

Prestigious tasks were assigned to him. In 1248 he was charged with opening a theological *studium* at Cologne, one of the most important regional capitals of Germany, where he lived at different times and which became his adopted city. He brought with him from Paris an exceptional student, Thomas Aquinas. The sole merit of having been Saint Thomas' teacher would suffice to elicit profound admiration for Saint Albert. A relationship of mutual esteem and friendship developed between these two great theologians, human attitudes that were very helpful in the development of this branch of knowledge. In 1254, Albert was elected Provincial of the Dominican Fathers' "Provincia Teutoniae"—Teutonic Province—which included communities scattered over a vast territory in Central and Northern Europe. He distinguished himself for the zeal with which he exercised this ministry, visiting the communities and constantly recalling his confreres to fidelity, to the teaching and example of Saint Dominic.

His gifts did not escape the attention of the Pope of that time, Alexander IV, who wanted Albert with him for a certain time at Anagni—where the Popes went frequently—in Rome itself, and at Viterbo, in order to avail himself of Albert's theological advice. The same Supreme Pontiff appointed Albert Bishop of Regensburg, a large and celebrated diocese, but which was going through a difficult period. From 1260 to 1262, Albert exercised this ministry with unflagging dedication, succeeding in restoring peace and harmony to the city, in reorganizing parishes and convents, and in giving a new impetus to charitable activities.

In the year 1263–1264, Albert preached in Germany and in Bohemia, at the request of Pope Urban IV. He later returned to Cologne and took up his role as lecturer, scholar, and writer. As a man of prayer, science, and charity, his authoritative intervention in various events of the Church and of the society of the time were acclaimed: above all, he was a man of reconciliation and peace in Cologne, where the Archbishop had run seriously foul of the city's institutions; he did his utmost during the Second Council of Lyons, in 1274, summoned by Pope Gregory X, to encourage union between the Latin and Greek Churches after the separation of the great schism with the East in 1054. He also explained the thought of Thomas Aquinas, which had been the subject of objections and even quite unjustified condemnations.

He died in his cell at the convent of the Holy Cross, Cologne, in 1280, and was very soon venerated by his confreres. The Church proposed him for the worship of the faithful with his beatification in 1622 and with his canonization in 1931, when Pope Pius XI proclaimed him Doctor of the Church. This was certainly an appropriate recognition of this great man of God and outstanding scholar, not only of the truths of the faith but of a great many other branches of knowledge; indeed, with a glance at the titles of his very numerous works, we realize that there was something miraculous about his culture and that his encyclopedic interests led him to concern himself not only with philosophy and theology, like other contemporaries of his, but also with every other discipline then known, from physics to chemistry, from astronomy to minerology, from botany to zoology. For this reason, Pope Pius XII named him Patron of enthusiasts of the natural sciences and also called him "Doctor universalis" precisely because of the vastness of his interests and knowledge.

Of course, the scientific methods that Saint Albert the Great used were not those that came to be established in the following centuries. His method consisted simply in the observation, description, and classification of the phenomena he had studied, but it was in this way that he opened the door for future research.

He still has a lot to teach us. Above all, Saint Albert shows that there is no opposition between faith and science, despite certain episodes of misunderstanding that have been recorded in history. A man of faith and prayer, as was Saint Albert the Great, can serenely foster the study of the natural sciences and progress in knowledge of the micro- and macrocosm, discovering the laws proper to the subject, since all this contributes to fostering thirst for and love of God. The Bible speaks to us of creation as of the first language through which God—who is supreme intelligence, who is the Logos—reveals to us something of himself. The

Book of Wisdom, for example, says that the phenomena of nature, endowed with greatness and beauty, are like the works of an artist through which, by analogy, we may know the Author of creation (cf. Wis 13:5). With a classical similitude in the Middle Ages and in the Renaissance, one can compare the natural world to a book written by God that we read according to the different approaches of the sciences (cf. *Address to the Participants in the Plenary Meeting of the Pontifical Academy of Sciences*, 31 October 2008; *L'Osservatore Romano English edition*, 5 November 2008, p. 6). How many scientists, in fact, in the wake of Saint Albert the Great, have carried on their research inspired by wonder at and gratitude for a world which, to their eyes as scholars and believers, appeared and appears as the good work of a wise and loving Creator! Scientific study is then transformed into a hymn of praise. Enrico Medi, a great astrophysicist of our time, whose cause of beatification has been introduced, wrote:

> O you mysterious galaxies ... I see you, I calculate you, I understand you, I study you and I discover you, I penetrate you and I gather you. From you I take light and make it knowledge, I take movement and make it wisdom, I take sparkling colors and make them poetry; I take you stars in my hands and, trembling in the oneness of my being, I raise you above yourselves and offer you in prayer to the Creator, that through me alone you stars can worship. (*Le Opere. Inno alla creazione.*)

Saint Albert the Great reminds us that there is friendship between science and faith and that through their vocation to the study of nature, scientists can take an authentic and fascinating path of holiness.

His extraordinary openmindedness is also revealed in a cultural feat which he carried out successfully, that is, the acceptance and appreciation of Aristotle's thought. In Saint Albert's time, in fact, knowledge was spreading of numerous works by this great Greek philosopher, who lived a quarter of a century before Christ, especially in the sphere of ethics and metaphysics. They showed the power of reason, explained lucidly and clearly the meaning and structure of reality, its intelligibility, and the value and purpose of human actions. Saint Albert the Great opened the door to the complete acceptance in medieval philosophy and theology of Aristotle's philosophy, which was subsequently given a definitive form by Saint Thomas. This reception of a pagan pre-Christian philosophy, let us say, was an authentic cultural revolution in that epoch. Yet many Christian thinkers feared Aristotle's philosophy, a non-Christian philosophy, especially because, presented by his Arab commentators, it had been interpreted in such a way, at least in certain points, as to appear completely irreconcilable with the Christian faith. Hence a dilemma arose: are faith and reason in conflict with each other or not?

This is one of the great merits of Saint Albert: with scientific rigor he studied Aristotle's works, convinced that all that is truly rational is compatible with the faith revealed in the Sacred Scriptures. In other words, Saint Albert the Great thus contributed to the formation of an autonomous philosophy, distinct from theology and united with it only by the unity of the truth. So it was that in the thirteenth century a clear distinction came into being between these two branches of knowledge, philosophy and theology, which, in conversing with each other, cooperate harmoniously in the discovery of the authentic vocation of man, thirsting for truth and happiness: and it is above all theology, which Saint Albert defined as "scientia affectiva" (affective knowledge), that points out to man his vocation to eternal joy, a joy that flows from full adherence to the truth.

Saint Albert the Great was capable of communicating these concepts in a simple and understandable way. An authentic son of Saint Dominic, he willingly preached to the People of God, who were won over by his words and by the example of his life.

Dear brothers and sisters, let us pray the Lord that learned theologians will never be lacking in holy Church, wise and devout like Saint Albert the Great, and that he may help each one of us to make our own the "formula of holiness" that he followed in his life: "to desire all that I desire for the glory of God, as God desires for his glory all that he desires", in other words, always to be conformed to God's will, in order to desire and to do everything only and always for his glory.

9

Saint Thomas Aquinas (1)

WEDNESDAY, 2 JUNE 2010
Saint Peter's Square

Dear Brothers and Sisters,

After several Catecheses on the priesthood and on my latest Journeys, today we return to our main theme: meditation on some of the great thinkers of the Middle Ages. We recently looked at the great figure of Saint Bonaventure, a Franciscan, and today I wish to speak of the one whom the Church calls the *Doctor communis*, namely, Saint Thomas Aquinas. In his Encyclical *Fides et Ratio*, my venerable Predecessor, Pope John Paul II, recalled that "the Church has been justified in consistently proposing Saint Thomas as a master of thought and a model of the right way to do theology" (no. 43). It is not surprising that, after Saint Augustine, among the ecclesiastical writers mentioned in the *Catechism of the Catholic Church*, Saint Thomas is cited more than any other, at least sixty-one times! He was also called the *Doctor Angelicus*, perhaps because of his virtues and, in particular, the sublimity of his thought and the purity of his life.

Thomas was born between 1224 and 1225 in the castle that his wealthy noble family owned at Roccasecca near Aquino, not far from the famous Abbey of Montecassino, where his parents sent him to receive the first elements of his education. A few years later, he moved to Naples, the capital of the Kingdom of Sicily, where Frederick II had founded a prestigious university. Here the thinking of the Greek philosopher Aristotle was taught without the limitations imposed elsewhere. The young Thomas was introduced to it and immediately perceived its great value. However, it was above all in those years that he spent in Naples that his Dominican vocation was born. Thomas was in fact attracted by the ideal of the Order recently founded by Saint Dominic. However, when he was clothed in the Dominican habit, his family opposed this decision, and he was obliged to leave the convent and spend some time at home.

In 1245, by which time he had come of age, he was able to continue on the path of his response to God's call. He was sent to Paris to study theology under the guidance of another saint, Albert the Great, of whom I spoke not long ago. A true and deep friendship developed between Albert and Thomas. They learned to esteem and love each other to the point that Albert even wanted his disciple to follow him to Cologne, where he had been sent by the Superiors of the Order to found a theological *studium*. Thomas then once again came into contact with all Aristotle's works and his Arab commentators, which Albert described and explained.

In this period the culture of the Latin world was profoundly stimulated by the encounter with Aristotle's works, which had long remained unknown. They were writings on the nature of knowledge, on the natural sciences, on metaphysics, on the soul, and on ethics and were full of information and intuitions that appeared valid and convincing. All this formed an overall vision of the world that had been developed without and before Christ, by means of pure reason, and seemed to impose itself on reason as "the" vision itself; accordingly, seeing and knowing this philosophy had an incredible fascination for the young. Many accepted enthusiastically, indeed, with a-critical enthusiasm, this enormous fund of ancient knowledge that seemed to be able to renew culture advantageously and to open totally new horizons. Others, however, feared that Aristotle's pagan thought might be in opposition to the Christian faith and refused to study it. Two cultures converged: the pre-Christian culture of Aristotle with its radical rationality and the classical Christian culture. Certain circles, moreover, were led to reject Aristotle by the presentation of this philosopher which had been made by the Arab commentators Avicenna and Averroës. Indeed, it was they who had transmitted the Aristotelian philosophy to the Latin world. For example, these commentators had taught that men have no personal intelligence but that there is a single universal intelligence, a spiritual substance common to all, that works in all as "one": hence, a depersonalization of man. Another disputable point passed on by the Arab commentators was that the world was eternal like God. This understandably unleashed never-ending disputes in the university and clerical worlds. Aristotelian philosophy was continuing to spread even among the populace.

Thomas Aquinas, at the school of Albert the Great, did something of fundamental importance for the history of philosophy and theology, I would say for the history of culture: he made a thorough study of Aristotle and his interpreters, obtaining for himself new Latin translations of the original Greek texts. Consequently he no longer relied solely on the Arab commentators but was able to read the original texts for himself. He commented on most of the Aristotelian opus, distinguishing between what was valid and what was dubious or to be completely rejected, showing its consonance with the events of Christian revelation and drawing abundantly and perceptively from Aristotle's thought in the explanation of the theological texts he was uniting. In short, Thomas Aquinas showed that a natural harmony exists between Christian faith and reason. And this was the great achievement of Thomas, who, at that time of clashes between two cultures—that time when it seemed that faith would have to give in to reason—showed that they go hand in hand, that insofar as reason appeared incompatible with faith, it was not reason and that what appeared to be faith was not faith if it was in opposition to true rationality; thus he created a new synthesis which formed the culture of the centuries to come.

Because of his excellent intellectual gifts, Thomas was summoned to Paris to be professor of theology on the Dominican chair. Here he began his literary production, which continued until his death and has something miraculous about it: he commented on Sacred Scripture because the professor of theology was above all an interpreter of Scripture; and he commented on the writings of Aristotle, powerful systematic works, among which stands out his *Summa Theologiae*, treatises and discourses on various subjects. He was assisted in the composition of his writings by several secretaries, including his confrere Reginald of Piperno, who followed him faithfully and to whom he was bound by a sincere brotherly friendship marked by great confidence and trust. This is a characteristic of saints: they cultivate friendship because it is one of the noblest manifestations of the human heart and has something divine about it, just as Thomas himself explained in some of the *Quaestiones* of his *Summa Theologiae*. He writes in it: "It is evident that charity is the friendship of man for God" and for "all belonging to him" (vol. II, q. 23, a. 1).

He did not stay long or permanently in Paris. In 1259 he took part in the General Chapter of the Dominicans in Valenciennes, where he was a member of a commission that established the Order's program of studies. Then from 1261 to 1265, Thomas was in Orvieto. Pope Urban IV, who held him in high esteem, commissioned him to compose liturgical texts for the Feast of *Corpus Christi*, which we are celebrating tomorrow, established subsequent to the Eucharistic miracle of Bolsena. Thomas had an exquisitely Eucharistic soul. The most beautiful hymns that the liturgy of the Church sings to celebrate the mystery of the Real Presence of the Body and Blood of the Lord in the Eucharist are attributed to his faith and his theological wisdom. From 1265 until 1268, Thomas lived in Rome, where he probably directed a *studium*, that is, a study house of his Order, and where he began writing his *Summa Theologiae* (cf. Jean-Pierre Torrell, *Tommaso d'Aquino. L'uomo e il teologo*, Casale Monf., 1994, pp. 118–84).

In 1269 Thomas was recalled to Paris for a second cycle of lectures. His students understandably were enthusiastic about his lessons. One of his former pupils declared that a vast multitude of students took Thomas' courses, so many that the halls could barely accommodate them; and this student added, making a personal comment, that "listening to him brought him deep happiness." Thomas' interpretation of Aristotle was not accepted by all, but even his adversaries in the academic field, such as Godfrey of Fontaines, for example, admitted that the teaching of Friar Thomas was superior to others for its usefulness and value and served to correct that of all the other masters. Perhaps also in order to distance him from the lively discussions that were going on, his Superiors sent him once again to Naples to be available to King Charles I, who was planning to reorganize university studies.

In addition to study and teaching, Thomas also dedicated himself to preaching to the people. And the people, too, came willingly to hear him. I would say that it is truly a great grace when theologians are able to speak to the faithful with simplicity and fervor. The ministry of preaching, moreover, helps theology scholars themselves to have a healthy pastoral realism and enriches their research with lively incentives.

The last months of Thomas' earthly life remain surrounded by a particular, I would say, mysterious atmosphere. In December 1273, he summoned his friend and secretary Reginald to inform him of his decision to discontinue all work because he had realized, during the celebration of Mass subsequent to a supernatural revelation, that everything he had written until then "was worthless". This is a mysterious episode that helps us to understand not only Thomas' personal humility, but also the fact that, however lofty and pure it may be, all we manage to think and say about the faith is infinitely exceeded by God's greatness and beauty, which will be fully revealed to us in Heaven. A few months later, more and more absorbed in thoughtful meditation, Thomas died while on his way to Lyons to take part in the Ecumenical Council convoked by Pope Gregory X. He died in the Cistercian Abbey of Fossanova, after receiving the Viaticum with deeply devout sentiments.

The life and teaching of Saint Thomas Aquinas could be summed up in an episode passed down by his ancient biographers. While, as was his wont, the Saint was praying before the Crucifix in the early morning in the chapel of Saint Nicholas in Naples, Domenico da Caserta, the church sacristan, overheard a conversation. Thomas was anxiously asking whether what he had written on the mysteries of the Christian faith was correct. And the Crucified One answered him: "You have spoken well of me, Thomas. What is your reward to be?" And the answer Thomas gave him was what we, too, friends and disciples of Jesus, always want to tell him: "Nothing but yourself, Lord!" (*Ibid.*, p. 320).

10

Saint Thomas Aquinas (2)

WEDNESDAY, 16 JUNE 2010
Saint Peter's Square

Dear Brothers and Sisters,

Today I would like to continue the presentation of Saint Thomas Aquinas, a theologian of such value that the study of his thought was explicitly recommended by the Second Vatican Council in two documents, the Decree *Optatam totius*, on the Training of Priests, and the Declaration *Gravissimum Educationis*, which addresses Christian Education. Indeed, already in 1880 Pope Leo XIII, who held Saint Thomas in high esteem as a guide and encouraged Thomistic studies, chose to declare him Patron of Catholic Schools and Universities.

The main reason for this appreciation is explained not only by the content of his teaching but also by the method he used, especially his new synthesis of and distinction between philosophy and theology. The Fathers of the Church were confronted by different philosophies of a Platonic type in which a complete vision of the world and of life was presented, including the subject of God and of religion. In comparison with these philosophies, they themselves had worked out a complete vision of reality, starting with faith and using elements of Platonism to respond to the essential questions of man. They called this vision, based on biblical revelation and formulated with a correct Platonism in the light of faith: "our philosophy". The word "philosophy" was not, therefore, an expression of a purely rational system and, as such, distinct from faith but rather indicated a comprehensive vision of reality, constructed in the light of faith but used and conceived of by reason; a vision that naturally exceeded the capacities proper to reason but as such also fulfilled it. For Saint Thomas, the encounter with the pre-Christian philosophy of Aristotle (who died in about 322 B.C.) opened up a new perspective. Aristotelian philosophy was obviously a philosophy worked out without the knowledge of the Old and New Testaments, an explanation of the world without revelation through reason alone. And this consequent rationality was convincing. Thus the old form of the Fathers' "our philosophy" no longer worked. The relationship between philosophy and theology, between faith and reason, needed to be rethought. A "philosophy" existed that was complete and convincing in itself, a rationality that preceded the faith, followed by "theology", a form of thinking with the faith and in the faith. The pressing question was this: are the world of rationality, philosophy conceived of without Christ, and the world of faith compatible? Or are they mutually exclusive? Elements that affirmed the incompatibility of these two worlds were not lacking, but Saint Thomas was firmly convinced of their compatibility—indeed, that philosophy worked out without the knowledge of Christ was awaiting, as it were, the light of Jesus to be complete. This was the great "surprise" of Saint Thomas that determined the path he took as a thinker. Showing this independence of philosophy and theology and, at the same time, their reciprocal relationality was the historic mission of the great teacher. And thus it can be understood that in the nineteenth century, when the incompatibility of modern reason and faith was strongly declared, Pope Leo XIII pointed to Saint Thomas as a guide in the dialogue between them. In his theological work, Saint Thomas supposes and concretizes this relationality. Faith consolidates, integrates, and illumines the heritage of truth that human reason acquires. The trust with which Saint Thomas endows these two instruments of knowledge—faith and reason—may be traced back to the conviction that both stem from the one source of all truth, the divine *Logos*, which is active in both contexts, that of creation and that of redemption.

Together with the agreement between reason and faith, we must recognize, on the other hand, that they avail themselves of different cognitive procedures. Reason receives a truth by virtue of its intrinsic evidence, mediated or unmediated; faith, on the contrary, accepts a truth on the basis of the authority of the Word of God that is revealed. Saint Thomas writes at the beginning of his *Summa Theologiae*:

> We must bear in mind that there are two kinds of sciences. There are some which proceed from a principle known by the natural light of the intelligence, such as arithmetic and geometry and the like. There are some which proceed from principles known by the light of a higher science: thus the science of perspective proceeds from principles established by geometry, and music from principles established by arithmetic. So it is that sacred doctrine is a science, because it proceeds from principles established by the light of a higher science, namely, the science of God and the blessed. (Ia, q. 1, a.2.)

This distinction guarantees the autonomy of both the human and the theological sciences. However, it is not equivalent to separation but, rather, implies a reciprocal and advantageous collaboration. Faith, in fact, protects reason from any temptation to distrust its own abilities, stimulates it to be open to ever broader horizons, keeps alive in it the search for foundations, and, when reason itself is applied to the supernatural sphere of the relationship between God and man, faith enriches its work. According to Saint Thomas, for example, human reason can certainly reach the affirmation of the existence of one God, but only faith, which receives the divine revelation, is able to draw from the mystery of the Love of the triune God.

Moreover, it is not only faith that helps reason. Reason, too, with its own means can do something important for faith, making it a threefold service which Saint Thomas sums up in the preface to his commentary on the *De Trinitate* of Boethius: "demonstrating those truths that are preambles of the faith; giving a clearer notion, by certain similitudes, of the truths of the faith; resisting those who speak against the faith, either by showing that their statements are false or by showing that they are not necessarily true" (q. 2, a. 3). The entire history of theology is basically the exercise of this task of the mind, which shows the intelligibility of faith, its articulation and inner harmony, its reasonableness and its ability to further human good. The correctness of theological reasoning and its real cognitive meaning is based on the value of theological language, which, in Saint Thomas' opinion, is principally an analogical language. The distance between God, the Creator, and the being of his creatures is infinite; dissimilitude is ever greater than similitude (cf. DS 806). Nevertheless, in the whole difference between Creator and creatures an analogy exists between the created being and the being of the Creator, which enables us to speak about God with human words.

Saint Thomas based the doctrine of analogy not only on exceptional philosophical argumentation but also on the fact that with revelation God himself spoke to us and therefore authorized us to speak of him. I consider it important to recall this doctrine. In fact, it helps us get the better of certain objections of contemporary atheism, which denies that religious language is provided with an objective meaning and instead maintains that it has solely a subjective or merely emotional value. This objection derives from the fact that positivist thought is convinced that man does not know being but solely the functions of reality that can be experienced. With Saint Thomas and with the great philosophical tradition we are convinced that, in reality, man does not only know the functions, the object of the natural sciences, but also knows something of being itself—for example, he knows the person, the You of the other, and not only the physical and biological aspect of his being.

In the light of this teaching of Saint Thomas, theology says that however limited it may be, religious language is endowed with sense because we touch being like an arrow aimed at the reality it signifies. This fundamental agreement between human reason and Christian faith is recognized in another basic principle of Aquinas' thought. Divine grace does not annihilate but presupposes and perfects human nature. The latter, in fact, even after sin, is not completely corrupt but wounded and weakened. Grace, lavished upon us by God and communicated through the mystery of the Incarnate Word, is an absolutely free gift with which nature is healed, strengthened, and assisted in pursuing the innate desire for happiness in the heart of every man and of every woman. All the faculties of the human being are purified, transformed, and uplifted by divine grace.

An important application of this relationship between nature and grace is recognized in the moral theology of Saint Thomas Aquinas, which proves to be of great timeliness. At the center of his teaching in this field, he places the new law, which is the law of the Holy Spirit. With a profoundly evangelical gaze, he insists on the fact that this law is the grace of the Holy Spirit given to all who believe in Christ. The written and oral teaching of the doctrinal and moral truths transmitted by the Church is united to this grace. Saint Thomas, emphasizing the fundamental role in moral life of the action of the Holy Spirit, of grace, from which flow the theological and moral virtues, makes us understand that all Christians can attain the lofty perspectives of the "Sermon on the Mount" if they live an authentic relationship of faith in Christ, if they are open to the action of his Holy Spirit. However, Aquinas adds, "Although grace is more efficacious than nature, yet nature is more essential to man and, therefore, more enduring" (*Summa Theologiae*, Ia–IIae, q. 94, a. 6 ad 2), which is why, in the Christian moral perspective, there is a place for reason, which is capable of discerning natural moral law. Reason can recognize this by considering what it is good to do and what it is good to avoid in order to achieve that felicity which everyone has at heart, which also implies a responsibility toward others and, therefore, the search for the common good. In other words, the human, theological, and moral virtues are rooted in human nature. Divine grace accompanies, sustains, and impels ethical commitment, but, according to Saint Thomas, all men, believers and non-believers alike, are called to recognize the needs of human nature expressed in natural law and to draw inspiration from it in the formulation of positive laws, namely, those issued by the civil and political authorities to regulate human coexistence.

When natural law and the responsibility it entails are denied, this dramatically paves the way to ethical relativism at the individual level and to totalitarianism of the State at the political level. The defense of universal human rights and the affirmation of the absolute value of the person's dignity postulate a foundation. Does not natural law constitute this foundation, with the non-negotiable values that it indicates? Venerable John Paul II wrote in his Encyclical *Evangelium Vitae* words that are still very up to date: "It is therefore urgently necessary, for the future of society and the development of a sound democracy, to rediscover those essential and innate human and moral values which flow from the very truth of the human being and express and safeguard the dignity of the person: values which no individual, no majority, and no State can ever create, modify, or destroy, but must only acknowledge, respect, and promote" (no. 71).

To conclude, Thomas presents to us a broad and confident concept of human reason: *broad* because it is not limited to the spaces of the so-called "empirical-scientific" reason, but open to the whole being and thus also to the fundamental and inalienable questions of human life; and *confident* because human reason, especially if it accepts the inspirations of Christian faith, is a promoter of a civilization that recognizes the dignity of the person, the inviolability of his rights and the cogency of his duties. It is not surprising that the doctrine on the dignity of the person, fundamental for the recognition of the inviolability of human rights, developed in schools of thought that accepted the legacy of Saint Thomas Aquinas, who had a very lofty conception of the human creature. He defined it, with his rigorously philosophical language, as "what is most perfect to be found in all nature—that is, a subsistent individual of a rational nature" (*Summa Theologiae*, Ia, q. 29, a. 3).

The depth of Saint Thomas Aquinas' thought—let us never forget it—flows from his living faith and fervent piety, which he expressed in inspired prayers such as this one in which he asks God: "Grant me, O Lord my God, a mind to know you, a heart to seek you, wisdom to find you, conduct pleasing to you, faithful perseverance in waiting for you, and a hope of finally embracing you."

11

Saint Thomas Aquinas (3)

WEDNESDAY, 23 JUNE 2010
Paul VI Hall

Dear Brothers and Sisters,

Today I would like to complete, with a third installment, my Catecheses on Saint Thomas Aquinas. Even more than seven hundred years after his death we can learn much from him. My Predecessor Pope Paul VI also said this, in a Discourse he gave at Fossanova on 14 September 1974 on the occasion of the seventh centenary of Saint Thomas' death. He asked himself: "Thomas, our Teacher, what lesson can you give us?" And he answered with these words: "Trust in the truth of Catholic religious thought, as defended, expounded, and offered by him to the capacities of the human mind" (*Address in Honor of Saint Thomas Aquinas in the Basilica*, 14 September 1974; *L'Osservatore Romano* English edition, [*ORE*], 26 September 1974, p. 4). In Aquino moreover, on that same day, again with reference to Saint Thomas, Paul VI said, "all of us who are faithful sons and daughters of the Church can and must be his disciples, at least to some extent!" (*Address to People in the Square at Aquino*, 14 September 1974; *ORE*, p. 5).

Let us too, therefore, learn from the teaching of Saint Thomas and from his masterpiece, the *Summa Theologiae*. It was left unfinished, yet it is a monumental work: it contains 512 questions and 2,669 articles. It consists of concentrated reasoning in which the human mind is applied with clarity and depth to the mysteries of faith, alternating questions with answers in which Saint Thomas deepens the teaching that comes from Sacred Scripture and from the Fathers of the Church, especially Saint Augustine. In this reflection, in meeting the true questions of his time, which are also often our own questions, Saint Thomas, also by employing the method and thought of the ancient philosophers, and of Aristotle in particular, thus arrives at precise, lucid, and pertinent formulations of the truths of faith, in which truth is a gift of faith, shines out, and becomes accessible to us, for our reflection. However, this effort of the human mind—Aquinas reminds us with his own life—is always illumined by prayer, by the light that comes from on high. Only those who live with God and with his mysteries can also understand what they say to us.

In the *Summa* of theology, Saint Thomas starts from the fact that God has three different ways of being and existing: God exists in himself, he is the beginning and end of all things, which is why all creatures proceed from him and depend on him; then God is present through his grace in the life and activity of the Christian, of the saints; lastly, God is present in an altogether special way in the Person of Christ, here truly united to the man Jesus, and active in the sacraments that derive from his work of redemption. Therefore, the structure of this monumental work (cf. Jean-Pierre Torrell, *La "Summa" di San Tommaso*, Milan, 2003, pp. 29–75), a quest with "a theological vision" for the fullness of God (cf. *Summa Theologiae*, Ia, q. 1, a. 7), is divided into three parts and is illustrated by the *Doctor Communis* himself—Saint Thomas—with these words: "Because the chief aim of sacred doctrine is to teach the knowledge of God, not only as he is in himself, but also as he is the beginning of things and their last end, and especially of rational creatures, as is clear from what has already been said, therefore, we shall treat: (1) Of God; (2) Of the rational creature's advance toward God; (3) Of Christ, who, as man, is our way to God" (*ibid.*, I, q. 2). It is a circle: God in himself, who comes out of himself and takes us by the hand, in such a way that with Christ we return to God, we are united to God, and God will be all things to all people.

The First Part of the *Summa Theologiae* thus investigates God in himself, the mystery of the Trinity and of the creative activity of God. In this part we also find a profound reflection on the authentic reality of man, inasmuch as he has emerged from the creative hands of God as the fruit of his love. On the one hand, we are dependent created beings, we do not come from ourselves; yet, on the other, we have a true autonomy so that we are not only something apparent—as certain Platonic philosophers say—but a reality desired by God as such and possessing an inherent value.

In the Second Part, Saint Thomas considers man, impelled by grace, in his aspiration to know and love God in order to be happy in time and in eternity. First of all, the Author presents the theological principles of moral action, studying how, in the free choice of men to do good acts, reason, will, and passions are integrated, to which is added the power given by God's grace through the virtues and the gifts of the Holy Spirit, as well as the help offered by moral law. Hence man is a dynamic being who seeks himself, seeks to become himself, and, in this regard, seeks to do actions that build him up, that make him truly man; and here the moral law comes into it. Grace and reason itself, the will and the passions enter, too. On this basis, Saint Thomas describes the profile of the man who lives in accordance with the Spirit and thus becomes an image of God. Here Aquinas pauses to study the three theological virtues—faith, hope, and charity—followed by a critical examination of more than fifty moral virtues, organized around the four cardinal virtues: prudence, justice, temperance, and fortitude. He then ends with a reflection on the different vocations in the Church.

In the Third Part of the *Summa*, Saint Thomas studies the mystery of Christ—the way and the truth—through which we can reach God the Father. In this section he writes almost unparalleled pages on the mystery of Jesus' Incarnation and Passion, adding a broad treatise on the seven sacraments, for it is in them that the Divine Word Incarnate extends the benefits of the Incarnation for our salvation, for our journey of faith toward God and eternal life. He is, as it were, materially present with the realities of creation and, thus, touches us in our inmost depths.

In speaking of the sacraments, Saint Thomas reflects in a special way on the mystery of the Eucharist, for which he had such great devotion, the early biographers claim, that he would lean his head against the Tabernacle, as if to feel the throbbing of Jesus' divine and human heart. In one of his works, commenting on Scripture, Saint Thomas helps us to understand the excellence of the sacrament of the Eucharist, when he writes: "Since this [the Eucharist] is the sacrament of our Lord's Passion, it contains in itself the Jesus Christ who suffered for us. Thus, whatever is an effect of our Lord's Passion is also an effect of this sacrament. For this sacrament is nothing other than the application of our Lord's Passion to us" (cf. *Commentary on John*, chap. 6, lecture 6, no. 963). We clearly understand why Saint Thomas and other saints celebrated Holy Mass shedding tears of compassion for the Lord who gave himself as a sacrifice for us, tears of joy and gratitude.

Dear brothers and sisters, at the school of the saints, let us fall in love with this sacrament! Let us participate in Holy Mass with recollection, to obtain its spiritual fruits, let us nourish ourselves with this Body and Blood of our Lord, to be ceaselessly fed by divine grace! Let us willingly and frequently linger in the company of the Blessed Sacrament in heart-to-heart conversation!

All that Saint Thomas described with scientific rigor in his major theological works, such as, precisely, the *Summa Theologiae* and the *Summa contra gentiles*, was also explained in his preaching, both to his students and to the faithful. In 1273, a year before he died, he preached throughout Lent in the Church of San Domenico Maggiore in Naples. The content of those sermons was gathered and preserved: they are the *Opuscula* in which he explains the *Apostles' Creed*, interprets the prayer of the *Our Father*, explains the *Ten Commandments*, and comments on the *Hail Mary*. The content of the *Doctor Angelicus'* preaching corresponds with virtually the whole structure of the *Catechism of the Catholic Church*. Actually, in catechesis and preaching, in a time like ours of renewed commitment to evangelization, these fundamental subjects should never be lacking: what *we believe*, and here is the Creed of the faith; what *we pray*, and here is the *Our Father* and the *Hail Mary;* and what *we live*, as we are taught by biblical revelation, and here is the law of the love of God and neighbor and the *Ten Commandments*, as an explanation of this mandate of love.

I would like to propose some simple, essential, and convincing examples of the content of Saint Thomas' teaching. In his booklet on *The Apostles' Creed*, he explains the value of faith. Through it, he says, the soul is united to

God; something like a nucleus of eternal life is formed; life receives a reliable orientation, and we overcome temptations with ease. To those who object that faith is foolishness because it leads to belief in something that does not come within the experience of the senses, Saint Thomas gives a very articulate answer and recalls that this is an inconsistent doubt, for human intelligence is limited and cannot know everything. Only if we were able to know all visible and invisible things perfectly would it be genuinely foolish to accept truths out of pure faith. Moreover, it is impossible to live, Saint Thomas observes, without trusting in the experience of others, wherever one's own knowledge falls short. It is thus reasonable to believe in God, who reveals himself, and to the testimony of the Apostles: they were few, simple, and poor, grief-stricken by the Crucifixion of their Teacher. Yet many wise, noble, and rich people converted very soon after hearing their preaching. In fact this is a miraculous phenomenon of history, to which it is far from easy to give a convincing answer other than that of the Apostles' encounter with the Risen Lord.

In commenting on the article of the Creed on the Incarnation of the Divine Word, Saint Thomas makes a few reflections. He says that the Christian faith is strengthened in considering the mystery of the Incarnation; hope is strengthened at the thought that the Son of God came among us, as one of us, to communicate his own divinity to men; charity is revived because there is no more obvious sign of God's love for us than the sight of the Creator of the universe making himself a creature, one of us. Finally, in contemplating the mystery of God's Incarnation, we feel kindled within us our desire to reach Christ in glory. Using a simple and effective comparison, Saint Thomas remarks: "If the brother of a king were to be far away, he would certainly long to live beside him. Well, Christ is a brother to us; we must therefore long for his company and become of one heart with him" (*Opuscoli teologico-spirituali*, Rome, 1976, p. 64).

In presenting the prayer of the *Our Father*, Saint Thomas shows that it is perfect in itself, since it has all five of the characteristics that a well-made prayer must possess: trusting, calm abandonment; a fitting content, because, Saint Thomas observes, "it is quite difficult to know exactly what it is appropriate and inappropriate to ask for, since choosing among our wishes puts us in difficulty" (*ibid.*, p. 120); and then an appropriate order of requests, the fervor of love, and the sincerity of humility.

Like all the saints, Saint Thomas had a great devotion to Our Lady. He described her with a wonderful title: *Triclinium totius Trinitatis; triclinium*, that is, a place where the Trinity finds rest since, because of the Incarnation, in no creature as in her do the three Divine Persons dwell and feel delight and joy at dwelling in her soul full of grace. Through her intercession we may obtain every help.

With a prayer that is traditionally attributed to Saint Thomas and that in any case reflects the elements of his profound Marian devotion, we too say: "O most Blessed and sweet Virgin Mary, Mother of God, . . . I entrust to your merciful heart . . . my entire life. . . . Obtain for me as well, O most sweet Lady, true charity with which from the depths of my heart I may love your most Holy Son, our Lord Jesus Christ, and, after him, love you above all other things . . . and my neighbor, in God and for God."

12

John Duns Scotus

WEDNESDAY, 7 JULY 2010
Paul VI Hall

Dear Brothers and Sisters,

This morning, after several Catecheses on various great theologians, I would like to present to you another important figure in the history of theology. He is Blessed John Duns Scotus, who lived at the end of the thirteenth century. An ancient epitaph on his tombstone sums up the geographical coordinates of his biography: "Scotland bore me, England received me, France taught me, Cologne in Germany holds me." We cannot disregard this information, partly because we know very little about the life of Duns Scotus. He was probably born in 1266 in a village called, precisely, "Duns", near Edinburgh. Attracted by the charism of Saint Francis of Assisi, he entered the Family of the Friars Minor and was ordained a priest in 1291. He was endowed with a brilliant mind and a tendency for speculation which earned him the traditional title of *Doctor subtilis*, "Subtle Doctor". Duns Scotus was directed to the study of philosophy and theology at the famous Universities of Oxford and of Paris. Having successfully completed his training, he embarked on teaching theology at the Universities of Oxford and Cambridge and then of Paris, beginning by commenting, like all the bachelors of theology of his time, on the *Sentences* of Peter Lombard. Indeed, Duns Scotus' main works are the mature fruit of these lessons and take the name of the places where he taught: *Ordinatio* (called in the past *Opus Oxoniense*—Oxford), *Reportatio Cantabrigiensis* (Cambridge), *Reportata Parisiensia* (Paris). One can add to these at least the *Quodlibeta* (or *Quaestiones quodlibetales*), a quite important work consisting of twenty-one questions on various theological subjects. Duns Scotus distanced himself from Paris, after a serious dispute broke out between King Philip IV the Fair and Pope Boniface VIII, preferring voluntary exile rather than sign a document hostile to the Supreme Pontiff as the King requested of all religious. Thus he left the country, together with the Franciscan friars, out of love for the See of Peter.

Dear brothers and sisters, this event invites us to remember how often in the history of the Church believers have met with hostility and even suffered persecution for their fidelity and devotion to Christ, to the Church, and to the Pope. We all look with admiration at these Christians, who teach us to treasure as a precious good faith in Christ and communion with the Successor of Peter, hence with the universal Church.

However, friendly relations between the King of France and the Successor of Boniface VIII were soon restored, and in 1305 Duns Scotus was able to return to Paris to lecture on theology with the title of *Magister regens* [regent master], now we would say "Professor". Later his Superiors sent him to Cologne as Professor of the Franciscan *Studium* of Theology, but he died on 8 November 1308, when he was only forty-three years old, leaving, nevertheless, a considerable number of works.

Because of the fame of his holiness, his cult soon became widespread in the Franciscan Order, and Venerable Pope

John Paul II, wishing to confirm it, solemnly beatified him on 20 March 1993, describing him as the "minstrel of the Incarnate Word and defender of Mary's Immaculate Conception" (*Solemn Vespers*, Saint Peter's Basilica; *L'Osservatore Romano* [ORE] English edition, no. 3, 24 March 1993, p. 1). These words sum up the important contribution that Duns Scotus made to the history of theology.

Above all, he meditated on the mystery of the Incarnation and, unlike many Christian thinkers of the time, held that the Son of God would have been made man even if mankind had not sinned. He says in his "*Reportatio Parisiensis*": "To think that God would have given up such a task had Adam not sinned would be quite unreasonable! I say, therefore, that the fall was not the cause of Christ's predestination and that—if no one had fallen, neither the angel nor man—in this hypothesis Christ would still have been predestined in the same way" (in *III Sent.*, d. 7, 4). This perhaps somewhat surprising thought crystallized because, in the opinion of Duns Scotus, the Incarnation of the Son of God, planned from all eternity by God the Father at the level of love, is the fulfillment of creation and enables every creature, in Christ and through Christ, to be filled with grace and to praise and glorify God in eternity. Although Duns Scotus was aware that in fact, because of original sin, Christ redeemed us with his Passion, death, and Resurrection, he reaffirmed that the Incarnation is the greatest and most beautiful work of the entire history of salvation, that it is not conditioned by any contingent fact but is God's original idea of ultimately uniting with himself the whole of creation, in the Person and Flesh of the Son.

As a faithful disciple of Saint Francis, Duns Scotus liked to contemplate and preach the mystery of the saving Passion of Christ as the expression of the loving will, of the immense love of God, who reaches out with the greatest generosity, irradiating his goodness and love (cf. *Tractatus de primo principio*, c. 4). Moreover, this love was revealed not only on Calvary but also in the Most Blessed Eucharist, for which Duns Scotus had a very deep devotion and which he saw as the sacrament of the Real Presence of Jesus and as the sacrament of unity and communion that induces us to love each other and to love God, as the Supreme Good we have in common (cf. *Reportatio Parisiensis*, in *IV Sent.*, d. 8, q. 1, n. 3). As I wrote in my Letter for the International Congress in Cologne marking the seventh centenary of the death of Blessed Duns Scotus, citing the thought of our author: "And as this love, this charity, was the origin of all things, so too our eternal happiness will be in love and charity alone: 'Eternal life is simply the desire as well as the will to love, blessed and perfect'" (*AAS* 101 [2009], 5).

Dear brothers and sisters, this strongly "Christocentric" theological vision opens us to contemplation, wonder, and gratitude: Christ is the center of history and of the cosmos; it is he who gives meaning, dignity, and value to our lives! As Pope Paul VI proclaimed in Manila, I too would like to cry out to the world: [Christ] "reveals the invisible God; he is the firstborn of all creation, the foundation of everything created. He is the Teacher of mankind and its Redeemer. He was born, he died, and he rose again for us. He is the center of history and of the world; he is the one who knows us and who loves us; he is the companion and the friend of our life. . . . I could never finish speaking about him" (*Homily*, Mass at Quezon Circle, Manila; 29 November 1970).

Not only Christ's role in the history of salvation but also that of Mary is the subject of the *Doctor subtilis'* thought. In the times of Duns Scotus, the majority of theologians opposed, with an objection that seemed insurmountable, the doctrine which holds that Mary Most Holy was exempt from original sin from the very first moment of her conception: in fact, at first sight the universality of the redemption brought about by Christ might seem to be jeopardized by such a statement, as though Mary had had no need of Christ or his redemption. Thus, to enable people to understand this preservation from original sin, Duns Scotus developed an argument that was later, in 1854, also to be used by Blessed Pope Pius IX when he solemnly defined the Dogma of the Immaculate Conception of Mary. And this argument is that of "preventive redemption", according to which the Immaculate Conception is the masterpiece of the redemption brought about by Christ because the very power of his love and his mediation obtained that the Mother be preserved from original sin. Therefore Mary is totally redeemed by Christ, but already before her conception. Duns Scotus' confreres, the Franciscans, accepted and spread this doctrine enthusiastically, and other theologians, often with a solemn oath, strove to defend and perfect it.

In this regard I would like to highlight a fact that I consider relevant. Concerning the teaching on the Immaculate Conception, important theologians like Duns Scotus enriched what the People of God already spontaneously believed about the Blessed Virgin and expressed in acts of devotion, in the arts, and in Christian life in general with the specific contribution of their thought. Thus faith both in the Immaculate Conception and in the bodily Assumption of the Virgin was already present in the People of God, while theology had not yet found the key to interpreting it in the totality of the doctrine of the faith. The People of God therefore precede theologians, and this is all thanks to that supernatural *sensus fidei*, namely, that capacity infused by the Holy Spirit that qualifies us to embrace the reality of the faith with humility of heart and mind. In this sense, the People of God is the "teacher that goes first" and must then be more deeply examined and intellectually accepted by theology. May theologians always be ready to listen to this source of faith and retain the humility and simplicity of children! I mentioned this a few months ago, saying:

> There have been great scholars, great experts, great theologians, teachers of faith who have taught us many things. They have gone into the details of Sacred Scripture . . . but have been unable to see the mystery itself, its central nucleus. . . . The essential has remained hidden! . . . On the other hand, in our time there have also been "little ones" who have understood this mystery. Let us think of Saint Bernadette Soubirous; of Saint Thérèse of Lisieux, with her new interpretation of the Bible that is "non-scientific" but goes to the heart of Sacred Scripture. (*Homily, Mass for the Members of the International Theological Commission*, Pauline Chapel, Vatican City, 1 December 2009.)

Lastly, Duns Scotus developed a point to which modernity is very sensitive. It is the topic of freedom and its relationship with the will and with the intellect. Our author underlines freedom as a fundamental quality of the will, introducing an approach that lays greater emphasis on the will. Unfortunately, in later authors, this line of thinking turned into a voluntarism, in contrast to the so-called "Augustinian and Thomist intellectualism". For Saint Thomas Aquinas, who follows Saint Augustine, freedom cannot be considered an innate quality of the will, but is the fruit of the collaboration of the will and the mind. Indeed, an idea of innate and absolute freedom—as it evolved, precisely, after Duns Scotus—placed in the will that precedes the intellect, both in God and in man, risks leading to the idea of a God who would not even be bound to truth and the good. The wish to save God's absolute transcendence and diversity with such a radical and impenetrable accentuation of his will does not take into account that the God who revealed himself in Christ is the God "Logos", who acted and acts full of love for us. Of course, as Duns Scotus affirms, love transcends knowledge and is capable of perceiving ever better than thought, but it is always the love of the God who is "Logos" (cf. Benedict XVI, *Address at the University of Regensburg*, 12 September 2006). In the human being, too, the idea of absolute freedom, placed in the will, forgetting the connection with the truth, does not know that freedom itself must be liberated from the limits imposed on it by sin. All the same, the Scotist vision does not fall into these extremes: for Duns Scotus, a free act is the result of the concourse of intellect and will, and if he speaks of a "primacy" of the will, he argues this precisely because the will always follows the intellect.

In speaking to Roman seminarians last year, I recalled that, "Since the beginning and throughout all time but especially in the modern age, freedom has been the great dream of mankind" (*Discourse at the Roman Major Seminary*, 20 February 2009). Indeed, in addition to our own daily experience, modern history actually teaches us that freedom is authentic and helps with building a truly human civilization only when it is reconciled with truth. If freedom is detached from truth, it becomes, tragically, a principle of the destruction of man's inner harmony, a source of the abuse of power by the strongest and the violent and a cause of suffering and sorrow. Freedom, like all the faculties with which man is endowed, increases and is perfected, Duns Scotus says, when man is open to God, making the most of the disposition to listen to his voice, which he calls *potentia oboedientiales*: when we listen to divine revelation, to the word of God, in order to accept it, a message reaches us that fills our life with light and hope and we are truly free.

Dear brothers and sisters, Blessed Duns Scotus teaches us that in our life the essential thing is to believe that God is close to us and loves us in Jesus Christ and, therefore, to cultivate a deep love for him and for his Church. We on earth are witnesses of this love. May Mary Most Holy help us to receive this infinite love of God which we will enjoy eternally to the full in Heaven, when our soul is at last united to God forever in the Communion of Saints.

13

Saint Hildegard of Bingen (1)

WEDNESDAY, 1 SEPTEMBER 2010

Papal Summer Residence, Castel Gandolfo

Dear Brothers and Sisters,

In 1988, on the occasion of the Marian Year, Venerable John Paul II wrote an Apostolic Letter entitled *Mulieris Dignitatem* on the precious role that women have played and play in the life of the Church. "The Church", one reads in it, "gives thanks for all the manifestations of the *feminine* 'genius' which have appeared in the course of history, in the midst of all peoples and nations; she gives thanks for all the charisms that the Holy Spirit distributes to women in the history of the People of God, for all the victories which she owes to their faith, hope, and charity: she gives thanks for all the fruits of feminine holiness" (no. 31).

Various female figures stand out for the holiness of their lives and the wealth of their teaching even in those centuries of history that we usually call the Middle Ages. Today I would like to begin to present one of them to you: Saint Hildegard of Bingen, who lived in Germany in the twelfth century. She was born in 1098, probably at Bermersheim, Rhineland, not far from Alzey, and died in 1179 at the age of eighty-one, in spite of having always been in poor health. Hildegard belonged to a large noble family, and her parents dedicated her to God from birth for his service. At the age of eight, she was offered for the religious state (in accordance with the Rule of Saint Benedict, chap. 59), and, to ensure that she received an appropriate human and Christian formation, she was entrusted to the care of the consecrated widow Uda of Gölklheim and then to Jutta of Spanheim, who had taken the veil at the Benedictine Monastery of Saint Disibodenberg. A small cloistered women's monastery was developing there that followed the Rule of Saint Benedict. Hildegard was clothed by Bishop Otto of Bamberg, and in 1136, upon the death of Mother Jutta, who had become the community *magistra* (Prioress), the sisters chose Hildegard to succeed her. She fulfilled this office by making the most of her gifts as a woman of culture and of lofty spirituality, capable of dealing competently with the organizational aspects of cloistered life. A few years later, partly because of the increasing number of young women who were knocking at the monastery door, Hildegard broke away from the dominating male monastery of Saint Disibodenburg with her community, taking it to Bingen, calling it after Saint Rupert, and here she spent the rest of her days. Her manner of exercising the ministry of authority is an example for every religious community: she inspired holy emulation in the practice of good to such an extent that, as time was to tell, both the mother and her daughters competed in mutual esteem and in serving each other.

During the years when she was superior of the Monastery of Saint Disibodenberg, Hildegard began to dictate the mystical visions that she had been receiving for some time to the monk Volmar, her spiritual director, and to Richardis di Strade, her secretary, a sister of whom she was very fond. As always happens in the life of true mystics, Hildegard too wanted to put herself under the authority of wise people to discern the origin of her visions, fearing that they were the product of illusions and did not come from God. She thus turned to a person who was most highly esteemed in the Church in those times: Saint Bernard of Clairvaux, of whom I have already spoken in several Catecheses. He calmed and encouraged Hildegard. However, in 1147 she received a further, very important approval. Pope Eugene III, who was presiding at a Synod in Trier, read a text dictated by Hildegard presented to him by Archbishop Henry of Mainz. The Pope authorized the mystic to write down her visions and to speak in public. From that moment Hildegard's spiritual prestige continued to grow, so that her contemporaries called her the "Teutonic prophetess". This, dear friends, is the seal of an authentic experience of the Holy Spirit, the source of every charism: the person endowed with supernatural gifts never boasts of them, never flaunts them, and, above all, shows complete obedience to the ecclesial authority. Every gift bestowed by the Holy Spirit is in fact intended for the edification of the Church and the Church, through her Pastors, recognizes its authenticity.

I shall speak again next Wednesday about this great woman, this "prophetess", who also speaks with great timeliness to us today, with her courageous ability to discern the signs of the times, her love for creation, her medicine, her poetry, her music, which today has been reconstructed, her love for Christ and for his Church, which was suffering in that period too, wounded also in that time by the sins of both priests and lay people and far better loved as the Body of Christ. Thus Saint Hildegard speaks to us; we shall speak of her again next Wednesday.

14

Saint Hildegard of Bingen (2)

WEDNESDAY, 8 SEPTEMBER 2010

Paul VI Hall

Dear Brothers and Sisters,

Today I would like to take up and continue my Reflection on Saint Hildegard of Bingen, an important female figure of the Middle Ages who was distinguished for her spiritual wisdom and the holiness of her life. Hildegard's mystical visions resemble those of the Old Testament prophets: expressing herself in the cultural and religious categories of her time, she interpreted the Sacred Scriptures in the light of God, applying them to the various circumstances of life. Thus all those who heard her felt the need to live a consistent and committed Christian lifestyle. In a letter to Saint Bernard, the mystic from the Rhineland confesses: "The vision fascinates my whole being: I do not see with the eyes of the body, but it appears to me in the spirit of the mysteries.... I recognize the deep meaning of what is expounded on in the Psalter, in the Gospels, and in other books, which have been shown to me in the vision. This vision burns like a flame in my breast and in my soul and teaches me to understand the text profoundly" (*Epistolarium pars prima I-XC: CCCM* 91).

Hildegard's mystical visions have a rich theological content. They refer to the principal events of salvation history and use a language for the most part poetic and symbolic. For example, in her best-known work, entitled *Scivias*, that is, "You know the ways", she sums up in thirty-five visions the events of the history of salvation from the creation of the world to the end of time. With the characteristic traits of feminine sensitivity, Hildegard develops at the very heart of her work the theme of the mysterious marriage between God and mankind that is brought about in the Incarnation. On the tree of the Cross take place the nuptials of the Son of God with the Church, his Bride, filled with grace and the ability to give new children to God, in the love of the Holy Spirit (cf. *Visio tertia: PL* 197, 453c).

From these brief references we already see that theology, too, can receive a special contribution from women because they are able to talk about God and the mysteries of faith using their own particular intelligence and sensitivity. I therefore encourage all those who carry out this service to do it with a profound ecclesial spirit, nourishing their own reflection with prayer and looking to the great riches, not yet fully explored, of the medieval mystic tradition, especially that represented by luminous models such as Hildegard of Bingen.

The Rhenish mystic is also the author of other writings, two of which are particularly important since, like *Scivias*, they record her mystical visions: they are the *Liber vitae meritorum* (Book of the merits of life) and the *Liber divinorum operum* (Book of the divine works), also called *De operatione Dei*. In the former she describes a unique and powerful vision of God, who gives life to the cosmos with his power and his light. Hildegard stresses the deep relationship that exists between man and God and reminds us that the whole creation, of which man is the summit, receives life from the Trinity. The work is centered on the relationship between virtue and vice, which is why man must face the daily challenge of vice that distances him on the way toward God and of virtue that benefits him. The invitation is to distance oneself from evil in order to glorify God and, after a virtuous existence, enter the life that consists "wholly of joy". In her second work, which many consider her masterpiece, she once again describes creation in its relationship with God and the centrality of man, expressing a strong Christocentrism with a biblical-Patristic flavor. The Saint, who presents five visions inspired by the Prologue of the Gospel according to Saint John, cites the words of the Son to the Father: "The whole task that you wanted and entrusted to me I have carried out successfully, and so here I am in you and you in me and we are one" (*Pars III, Visio X: PL* 197, 1025a).

Finally, in other writings Hildegard manifests the versatility of interests and cultural vivacity of the female monasteries of the Middle Ages, in a manner contrary to the prejudices which still weighed on that period. Hildegard took an interest in medicine and in the natural sciences as well as in music, since she was endowed with artistic talent. Thus she composed hymns, antiphons, and songs, gathered under the title: *Symphonia Harmoniae Caelestium Revelationum* (Symphony of the harmony of heavenly revelations), which were performed joyously in her monasteries, spreading an atmosphere of tranquility, and which have also come down to us. For her, the entire creation is a symphony of the Holy Spirit, who is in himself joy and jubilation.

The popularity that surrounded Hildegard impelled many people to seek her advice. It is for this reason that we have so many of her letters at our disposal. Many male and female monastic communities turned to her, as well as Bishops and abbots. And many of her answers still apply for us. For instance, Hildegard wrote these words to a community of women religious: "The spiritual life must be tended with great dedication. At first the effort is burdensome because it demands the renunciation of caprices of the pleasures of the flesh and of other such things. But if she lets herself be enthralled by holiness, a holy soul will find even contempt for the world sweet and lovable. All that is needed is to take care that the soul does not shrivel" (E. Gronau, *Hildegard: Vita di una donna profetica alle origini dell'età moderna*, Milan, 1996, p. 402). And when the Emperor Frederic Barbarossa caused a schism in the Church by supporting at least three anti-popes against Alexander III, the legitimate Pope, Hildegard did not hesitate, inspired by her visions, to remind him that even he, the Emperor, was subject to God's judgment. With fearlessness, a feature of every prophet, she wrote to the Emperor these words as spoken by God: "You will be sorry for this wicked conduct of the godless who despise me! Listen, O King, if you wish to live! Otherwise my sword will pierce you!" (*ibid.*, p. 412).

With the spiritual authority with which she was endowed, in the last years of her life Hildegard set out on journeys, despite her advanced age and the uncomfortable conditions of travel, in order to speak to the People of God. They all listened willingly, even when she spoke severely: they considered her a messenger sent by God. She called, above all, the monastic communities and the clergy to a life in conformity with their vocation. In a special way Hildegard countered the movement of German *cátari* (Cathars). They—*cátari* means literally "pure"—advocated a radical reform of the Church, especially to combat the abuses of the clergy. She harshly reprimanded them for seeking to subvert the very nature of the Church, reminding them that a true renewal of the ecclesial community is obtained with a sincere spirit of repentance and a demanding process of conversion, rather than with a change of structures. This is a message that we should never forget. Let us always invoke the Holy Spirit, so that he may inspire in the Church holy and courageous women, like Saint Hildegard of Bingen, who, developing the gifts they have received from God, make their own special and valuable contribution to the spiritual development of our communities and of the Church in our time.

15

Saint Clare of Assisi

WEDNESDAY, 15 SEPTEMBER 2010

Paul VI Hall

Dear Brothers and Sisters,

One of the best loved saints is without a doubt Saint Clare of Assisi, who lived in the thirteenth century and was a contemporary of Saint Francis. Her testimony shows us how indebted the Church is to courageous women, full of faith like her, who can give a crucial impetus to the Church's renewal.

So who was Clare of Assisi? To answer this question we possess reliable sources: not only the ancient biographies, such as that of Tommaso da Celano, but also the *Proceedings* of the cause of her canonization that the Pope promoted only a few months after Clare's death and that contain the depositions of those who had lived a long time with her.

Born in 1193, Clare belonged to a wealthy, aristocratic family. She renounced her noble status and wealth to live in humility and poverty, adopting the lifestyle that Francis of Assisi recommended. Although her parents were planning a marriage for her with some important figure, as was then the custom, Clare, with a daring act inspired by her deep desire to follow Christ and her admiration for Francis, at the age of eighteen left her family home and, in the company of a friend, Bona di Guelfuccio, made her way in secret to the Friars Minor at the little Church of the Portiuncula. It was the evening of Palm Sunday in 1211. In the general commotion, a highly symbolic act took place: while his companions lit torches, Francis cut off Clare's hair, and she put on a rough penitential habit. From that moment she had become the virgin bride of Christ, humble and poor, and she consecrated herself totally to him. Like Clare and her companions, down through history innumerable women have been fascinated by love for Christ, who, with the beauty of his Divine Person, fills their hearts. And the entire Church, through the mystical nuptial vocation of consecrated virgins, appears what she will be forever: the pure and beautiful Bride of Christ.

In one of the four letters that Clare sent to Saint Agnes of Prague, the daughter of the King of Bohemia who wished to follow in Christ's footsteps, she speaks of Christ, her beloved Spouse, with nuptial words that may be surprising but are nevertheless moving:

> When you have loved [him], you shall be chaste; when you have touched [him], you shall become purer; when you have accepted [him], you shall be a virgin. Whose power is stronger, whose generosity is more elevated, whose appearance more beautiful, whose love more tender, whose courtesy more gracious. In whose embrace you are already caught up; who has adorned your breast with precious stones . . . and placed on your head a golden crown as a sign [to all] of your holiness. (*First Letter to Blessed Agnes of Prague: FF*, 2862.)

Especially at the beginning of her religious experience, Clare found in Francis of Assisi not only a teacher whose instructions she could follow but also a brotherly friend. The friendship between these two Saints is a very beautiful and important aspect. Indeed, when two pure souls on fire with the same love for God meet, they find in their friendship with each other a powerful incentive to advance on the path of perfection. Friendship is one of the noblest and loftiest human sentiments, which divine grace purifies and transfigures. Like Saint Francis and Saint Clare, other saints, too, experienced profound friendship on the journey toward Christian perfection. Examples are Saint Francis de Sales and Saint Jane Frances de Chantal. And Saint Francis de Sales himself wrote: "It is a blessed thing to love on earth as we hope to love in Heaven, and to begin that friendship here which is to endure forever there. I am not now speaking of simple charity, a love due to all mankind, but of that spiritual friendship which binds souls together, leading them to share devotions and spiritual interests, so as to have but one mind between them" (*The Introduction to a Devout Life* III, 19).

After spending a period of several months at other monastic communities, resisting the pressure of her relatives, who did not at first approve of her decision, Clare settled with her first companions at the Church of San Damiano, where the Friars Minor had organized a small convent for them. She lived in this monastery for more than forty years, until her death in 1253. A first-hand description has come down to us of how these women lived in those years at the beginning of the Franciscan movement. It is the admiring account of Jacques de Vitry, a Flemish Bishop who came to Italy on a visit. He declared that he had encountered a large number of men and women of every social class who, having "left all things for Christ, fled the world. They called themselves Friars Minor and Sisters Minor [Lesser] and are held in high esteem by the Lord Pope and the Cardinals.... The women live together in various homes not far from the city. They receive nothing but live on the work of their own hands. And they are deeply troubled and pained at being honored more than they would like to be by both clerics and lay people" (*Letter of October 1216: FF*, 2205, 2207).

Jacques de Vitry had perceptively noticed a characteristic trait of Franciscan spirituality about which Clare was deeply sensitive: the radicalism of poverty associated with total trust in divine Providence. For this reason, she acted with great determination, obtaining from Pope Gregory IX, or, probably, already from Pope Innocent III, the so-called *Privilegium Paupertatis* (cf. *FF*, 3279). On the basis of this privilege, Clare and her companions at San Damiano could not possess any material property. This was a truly extraordinary exception in comparison with the canon law then in force, but the ecclesiastical authorities of that time permitted it, appreciating the fruits of evangelical holiness that they recognized in the way of life of Clare and her sisters. This shows that even in the centuries of the Middle Ages, the role of women was not secondary but, on the contrary, considerable. In this regard, it is useful to remember that Clare was the first woman in the Church's history to compose a written Rule, submitted for the Pope's approval, to ensure the preservation of Francis of Assisi's charism in all the communities of women—large numbers of which were already springing up in her time—that wished to draw inspiration from the example of Francis and Clare.

In the Convent of San Damiano, Clare practiced heroically the virtues that should distinguish every Christian: humility, a spirit of piety and penitence, and charity. Although she was the superior, she wanted to serve the sick sisters herself and joyfully subjected herself to the most menial tasks. In fact, charity overcomes all resistance, and whoever loves joyfully performs every sacrifice. Her faith in the Real Presence of Christ in the Eucharist was so great that twice a miracle happened. Simply by showing to them the Most Blessed Sacrament, she turned away the Saracen mercenaries, who were on the point of attacking the convent of San Damiano and pillaging the city of Assisi.

Such episodes, like other miracles whose memory lives on, prompted Pope Alexander IV to canonize her in 1255, only two years after her death, outlining her eulogy in the Bull on the Canonization of Saint Clare. In it we read: "How powerful was the illumination of this light, and how strong the brightness of this source of light. Truly this light was kept hidden in the cloistered life; and outside, it shone with gleaming rays; it was gathered together in a strict convent, and outside it spread throughout the world; it was guarded within, and it flowed forth outside; Clare in fact lay hidden, but her life was revealed to all. Clare was silent, but her fame was shouted out" (*FF*, 3284). And this is exactly how it was, dear friends: those who change the world for the better are holy; they transform it permanently, instilling in it the energies that only love inspired by the Gospel can elicit. The saints are mankind's great benefactors!

Saint Clare's spirituality, the synthesis of the holiness she proposed, is summed up in the fourth letter she wrote to Saint Agnes of Prague. Saint Clare used an image very widespread in the Middle Ages that dates back to Patristic times: the mirror. And she invited her friend in Prague to consider herself in that mirror of the perfection of every virtue which is the Lord himself. She wrote:

> Happy, indeed, is the one permitted to share in this sacred banquet so as to be joined with all the feelings of her heart (to Christ), whose beauty all the blessed hosts of the Heavens unceasingly admire, whose affection moves, whose

> contemplation invigorates, whose generosity fills, whose sweetness replenishes, whose remembrance pleasantly brings light, whose fragrance will revive the dead, and whose glorious vision will bless all the citizens of the heavenly Jerusalem, because the vision of him is the *splendor of everlasting glory, the radiance of everlasting light, and a mirror without tarnish.* Look into this mirror every day, O Queen, spouse of Jesus Christ, and continually examine your face in it, so that in this way you may adorn yourself completely, inwardly and outwardly.... In this mirror shine blessed poverty, holy humility, and charity beyond words.... (*Fourth Letter to Blessed Agnes of Prague*, *FF*, 2901–3.)

Grateful to God, who gives us saints who speak to our hearts and offer us an example of Christian life to imitate, I would like to end with the same words of blessing that Saint Clare composed for her Sisters and which the Poor Clares, who play a precious role in the Church with their prayer and with their work, still preserve today with great devotion. These are words in which the full tenderness of her spiritual motherhood emerges: "I give you my blessing now while living, and after my death, in as far as I may: nay, even more than I may, I call down on you all the blessings that the Father of mercies has bestowed and continues to bestow on his spiritual sons and daughters, both in Heaven and on earth, and with which a spiritual father and mother have blessed and will bless their spiritual sons and daughters. Amen" (*FF*, 2856).

16

Saint Matilda of Hackeborn

WEDNESDAY, 29 SEPTEMBER 2010
Saint Peter's Square

Dear Brothers and Sisters,

Today I want to talk to you about Saint Matilda of Hackeborn, one of the great figures of the convent of Helfta, who lived in the thirteenth century. Her sister, Saint Gertrude the Great, tells of the special graces that God granted to Saint Matilda in the sixth book of *Liber Specialis Gratiae* (Book of special grace), which states: "What we have written is very little in comparison with what we have omitted. We are publishing these things solely for the glory of God and the usefulness of our neighbor, for it would seem wrong to us to keep quiet about the many graces that Matilda received from God, not so much for herself, in our opinion, but for us and for those who will come after us" (Mechthild von Hackeborn, *Liber specialis gratiae* VI, 1).

This work was written by Saint Gertrude and by another sister of Helfta and has a unique story. At the age of fifty, Matilda went through a grave spiritual crisis as well as physical suffering. In this condition she confided to two of her sisters, who were friends, the special graces with which God had guided her since childhood. However, she did not know that they were writing it all down. When she found out, she was deeply upset and distressed. However, the Lord reassured her, making her realize that all that had been written was for the glory of God and for the benefit of her neighbor (cf. *ibid.*, II, 25; V, 20). This work, therefore, is the principal source of information on the life and spirituality of our Saint.

With her we are introduced into the family of the Baron of Hackeborn, one of the noblest, richest, and most powerful barons of Thuringia, related to the Emperor Frederick II, and we enter the convent of Helfta in the most glorious period of its history. The Baron had already given one daughter to the convent, Gertrude of Hackeborn (1231/1232—1291/1292). She was gifted with an outstanding personality. She was abbess for forty years, capable of giving the spirituality of the convent a particular hallmark and of bringing it to an extraordinary flourishing as the center of mysticism and culture, a school for scientific and theological training. Gertrude offered the nuns an intellectual training of a high standard that enabled them to cultivate a spirituality founded on Sacred Scripture, on the liturgy, on the Patristic tradition, and on the Cistercian Rule and spirituality, with a particular love for Saint Bernard of Clairvaux and William of Saint-Thierry. She was a real teacher, exemplary in all things, in evangelical radicalism and in apostolic zeal. Matilda, from childhood, accepted and enjoyed the spiritual and cultural atmosphere created by her sister, later giving it her own personal hallmark.

Matilda was born in 1241 or 1242 in the Castle of Helfta. She was the Baron's third daughter. When she was seven, she went with her mother to visit her sister Gertrude in the convent of Rodersdorf. She was so enchanted by this environment that she ardently desired to belong to it. She entered as a schoolgirl and in 1258 became a nun at the convent, which in the meantime had moved to Helfta, to the property of the Hackeborns. She was distinguished by her humility, her fervor, her friendliness, the clarity and the innocence of her life, and by the familiarity and intensity with which she lived her relationship with God, the Virgin, and the saints. She was endowed with lofty natural and spiritual qualities, such as "knowledge, intelligence, familiarity with the humanities, and a marvelously sweet voice: everything made her well-suited to be a true treasure for the convent from every point of view" (*ibid.*, *Proem.*). Thus when "God's nightingale", as she was called, was still very young, she became the principal of the convent's school, choir mistress, and novice mistress, offices that she fulfilled with talent and unflagging zeal, for the benefit not only of the nuns but of anyone who wanted to draw on her wisdom and goodness.

Illumined by the divine gift of mystic contemplation, Matilda wrote many prayers. She was a teacher of faithful doctrine and deep humility, a counselor, comforter, and guide in discernment. We read:

> She distributed doctrine in an abundance never previously seen at the convent, and alas, we are rather afraid that nothing like it will ever be seen again. The sisters would cluster around her to hear the word of God, as if she were a preacher. She was the refuge and consoler of all and, by a unique gift of God, was endowed with the grace of being able to reveal freely the secrets of the heart of each one. Many people not only in the convent but also outsiders, religious and lay people who came from afar, testified that this holy virgin had freed them from their afflictions and that they had never known such comfort as they found near her. Furthermore, she composed and taught so many prayers that if they were gathered together they would make a book larger than a Psalter. (*Ibid.*, VI, 1.)

In 1261 a five-year-old girl came to the convent. Her name was Gertrude. She was entrusted to the care of Matilda, just twenty years of age, who taught her and guided her in the spiritual life until she made her into not only an excellent disciple but also her confidante. In 1271 or 1272, Matilda of Magdeburg also entered the convent. So it was that this place took in four great women—two Gertrudes and two Matildas—the glory of German monasticism. During her long life, which she spent in the convent, Matilda was afflicted with continuous and intense bouts of suffering, to which she added the very harsh penances chosen for the conversion of sinners. In this manner she participated in the Lord's Passion until the end of her life (cf. *ibid.*, VI, 2). Prayer and contemplation were the life-giving *humus* of her existence: her revelations, her teachings, her service to her neighbor, her journey in faith and in love have their root and their context here. In the first book of the work *Liber Specialis Gratiae*, the nuns wrote down Matilda's confidences pronounced on the Feasts of the Lord, the saints, and, especially, of the Blessed Virgin. This Saint had a striking capacity for living the various elements of the liturgy, even the simplest, and bringing it into the daily life of the convent. Some of her images, expressions, and applications are at times distant from our sensibility today, but, if we were to consider monastic life and her task as mistress and choir mistress, we should grasp her rare ability as a teacher and educator who, starting from the liturgy, helped her sisters to live intensely every moment of monastic life.

Matilda gave an emphasis in liturgical prayer to the canonical hours, to the celebrations of Holy Mass, and, especially, to Holy Communion. Here she was often rapt in ecstasy in profound intimacy with the Lord in his most ardent and sweetest heart, carrying on a marvelous conversation in which she asked for inner illumination, while interceding in a special way for her community and her sisters. At the center are the mysteries of Christ, which the Virgin Mary constantly recommends to people so that they may walk on the path of holiness: "If you want true holiness, be close to my Son; he is holiness itself, which sanctifies all things" (*ibid.*, I, 40). The whole world, the Church, benefactors, and sinners were present in her intimacy with God. For her, Heaven and earth were united.

Her visions, her teachings, the events of her life are described in words reminiscent of liturgical and biblical language. In this way it is possible to comprehend her deep knowledge of Sacred Scripture, which was her daily bread. She had constant recourse to the Scriptures, making the most of the biblical texts read in the liturgy and drawing from them symbols, terms, countryside, images, and famous figures. She had a special love for the Gospel:

> The words of the Gospel were a marvelous nourishment for her and in her heart stirred feelings of such sweetness that, because of her enthusiasm, she was often unable to finish reading it. . . . The way in which she read those words was so fervent that it inspired devotion in everyone. Thus when she was singing in the choir, she was completely absorbed in God, uplifted by such ardor that she sometimes expressed her feelings in gestures. . . . On other occasions, since she was rapt in ecstasy, she did not hear those who were calling or touching her and came back with difficulty to the reality of the things around her. (*Ibid.*, VI, 1.)

In one of her visions, Jesus himself recommended the Gospel to her; opening the wound in his most gentle heart, he said to her: "Consider the immensity of my love: if you want to know it well, nowhere will you find it more clearly expressed than in the Gospel. No one has ever heard expressed stronger or more tender sentiments than these: *As my father has loved me, so I have loved you* (Jn 15:9)" (*ibid.*, I, 22).

Dear friends, personal and liturgical prayer and especially the Liturgy of the Hours and Holy Mass are at the root of Saint Matilda of Hackeborn's spiritual experience. In letting herself be guided by Sacred Scripture and nourished by the Bread of the Eucharist, she followed a path of close union with the Lord, ever in full fidelity to the Church. This is also a strong invitation to us to intensify our friendship with the Lord, especially through daily prayer and attentive, faithful, and active participation in Holy Mass. The liturgy is a great school of spirituality.

Her disciple Gertrude gives a vivid picture of Saint Matilda of Hackeborn's last moments. They were very difficult but illumined by the presence of the Blessed Trinity, of the Lord, of the Virgin Mary, and of all the saints, even Gertrude's sister by blood. When the time came in which the Lord chose to gather her to him, she asked him let her live longer in suffering for the salvation of souls, and Jesus was pleased with this further sign of her love.

Matilda was fifty-eight years old. The last leg of her journey was marked by eight years of serious illness. Her work and the fame of her holiness spread far and wide. When her time came, "the God of majesty . . . the one delight of the soul that loves him . . . sang to her: *Venite vos, benedicti Patris mei* . . . . Come, O you who are blessed by my Father, come receive the Kingdom . . . and he united her with his glory" (*ibid.*, VI, 8).

May Saint Matilda of Hackeborn commend us to the Sacred Heart of Jesus and to the Virgin Mary. She invites us to praise the Son with the heart of the Mother and to praise Mary with the heart of the Son: "I greet you, O most deeply venerated Virgin, in that sweetest of dews which from the heart of the Blessed Trinity spread within you; I greet you in the glory and joy in which you now rejoice forever, you who were chosen in preference to all the creatures of the earth and of Heaven even before the world's creation! Amen" (*ibid.*, I, 45).

17

Saint Gertrude the Great

WEDNESDAY, 6 OCTOBER 2010

Saint Peter's Square

Dear Brothers and Sisters,

Saint Gertrude the Great, of whom I would like to talk to you today, brings us once again this week to the Monastery of Helfta, where several of the Latin-German masterpieces of religious literature were written by women. Gertrude belonged to this world. She is one of the most famous mystics, the only German woman to be called "Great", because of her cultural and evangelical stature: her life and her thought had a unique impact on Christian spirituality. She was an exceptional woman, endowed with special natural talents and extraordinary gifts of grace, the most profound humility and ardent zeal for her neighbor's salvation. She was in close communion with God both in contemplation and in her readiness to go to the help of those in need.

At Helfta, she compared herself systematically, so to speak, with her teacher, Matilda of Hackeborn, of whom I spoke at last Wednesday's Audience. Gertrude came into contact with Matilda of Magdeburg, another medieval mystic, and grew up under the wing of Abbess Gertrude, motherly, gentle, and demanding. From these three sisters she drew precious experience and wisdom; she worked them into a synthesis of her own, continuing on her religious journey with boundless trust in the Lord. Gertrude expressed the riches of her spirituality not only in her monastic world, but also and above all in the biblical, liturgical, Patristic, and Benedictine contexts, with a highly personal hallmark and great skill in communicating.

Gertrude was born on 6 January 1256, on the Feast of the Epiphany, but nothing is known of her parents or of the place of her birth. Gertrude wrote that the Lord himself revealed to her the meaning of this first uprooting: "I have chosen to dwell in her because it delights me to see that everything that people love in her is my own work.... Therefore I have exiled her from all her relatives, so that there should be no one who would love her for the sake of the ties of blood, and that I may be the only reason why all her friends love her" (*The Herald of Divine Love* I, 16, New York, 1993, p. 85).

When she was five years old, in 1261, she entered the monastery for formation and education, a common practice in that period. Here she spent her whole life, the most important stages of which she herself points out. In her memoirs she recalls that the Lord cared for her with forbearing patience and infinite mercy, forgetting the years of her childhood, adolescence, and youth, which she spent, she wrote,

> In [such] blindness and stupidity it seems to me that I would have felt no remorse in following my instincts in all places and in everything—thoughts, words, and deeds—had you not prevented me from doing so, both by giving me an inborn loathing of evil and delight in well-doing, and by the correction and guidance of other people. And so I should have lived, like a pagan among pagans.... And yet, from infancy, in my fifth year to be precise, you chose me to be

formed among the most faithful of your friends, to live in the household of your holy religion. (*Ibid.*, II, 23, p. 128.)

Gertrude was an extraordinary student; she learned everything that can be learned of the sciences of the trivium and quadrivium, the education of that time; she was fascinated by knowledge and threw herself into secular studies with zeal and tenacity, achieving scholastic successes beyond every expectation. If we know nothing of her origins, she herself tells us about her youthful passions: literature, music, and song and the art of miniature painting captivated her. She had a strong, determined, ready, and impulsive temperament. She often says that she was negligent; she recognizes her shortcomings and humbly asks forgiveness for them. She also humbly asks for advice and prayers for her conversion. Some features of her temperament and faults were to accompany her to the end of her life, so as to amaze certain people who wondered why the Lord had favored her with such a special love.

From being a student she moved on to dedicate herself totally to God in monastic life, and for twenty years nothing exceptional occurred: study and prayer were her main activities. Because of her gifts, she shone out among the sisters; she persisted in deepening her knowledge in various fields. Nevertheless, during Advent of 1280 she began to feel disgusted with all this and realized the vanity of it all. On 27 January 1281, a few days before the Feast of the Purification of the Virgin, toward the hour of Compline in the evening, the Lord with his illumination dispelled her deep anxiety. With gentle sweetness he calmed the distress that anguished her, a torment that Gertrude saw even as a gift of God, "to destroy the tower of vanity and worldiness which I had set up in my pride, although, alas, I was—in vain—bearing the name and wearing the habit of a religious.

This was the way in which you sought to show me your salvation" (*ibid.*, II, 1, p. 95). She had a vision of a young man who, in order to guide her through the tangle of thorns that surrounded her soul, took her by the hand. In that hand Gertrude recognized "those bright jewels, his wounds, which have canceled all our debts" (*ibid.*), and, thus, recognized the One who saved us with his Blood on the Cross: Jesus.

From that moment, her life of intimate communion with the Lord was intensified, especially in the most important liturgical seasons—Advent-Christmas, Lent-Easter, the feasts of Our Lady—even when illness prevented her from going to the choir. This was the same liturgical *humus* as that of Matilda, her teacher; but Gertrude describes it with simpler, more linear images, symbols, and terms that are more realistic, and her references to the Bible, to the Fathers, and to the Benedictine world are more direct.

Her biographer points out two directions of what we might describe as her own particular "conversion": *in study*, with the radical passage from secular, humanistic studies to the study of theology, and in *monastic observance*, with the passage from a life that she describes as *negligent*, to the life of intense, mystical prayer, with exceptional missionary zeal. The Lord, who had chosen her from her mother's womb and who since her childhood had made her partake of the banquet of monastic life, called her again with his grace "from exterior occupations to interior ones, from the practice of bodily exercises to the pursuit of spiritual ones" (*ibid.*, I, 1, p. 53). Gertrude understood that she was remote from him, *in the region of unlikeness*, as she said with Augustine; that she had dedicated herself with excessive greed to liberal studies, to human wisdom, overlooking spiritual knowledge, depriving herself of the taste for true wisdom; she was then led to the mountain of contemplation, where she cast off her former self to be reclothed in the new.

> Her love of learning now became desire for knowledge of God. Never tired of pondering over the pages of all the books of Holy Scripture that she was able to obtain or acquire, she filled the coffers of her heart to the brim with the sweetest and most useful sentences of Holy Scripture. And so she was always ready with godly and edifying words to help those who came to consult her and to refute errors with the testimony of Holy Scripture in such a way that no one could demolish her arguments. (*Ibid.*)

Gertrude transformed all this into an apostolate: she devoted herself to writing and popularizing the truth of faith with clarity and simplicity, with grace and persuasion, serving the Church faithfully and lovingly so as to be helpful to and appreciated by theologians and devout people.

Little of her intense activity has come down to us, partly because of the events that led to the destruction of the Monastery of Helfta. In addition to *The Herald of Divine Love* and *The Revelations*, we still have her *Spiritual Exercises*, a rare jewel of mystical spiritual literature.

In religious observance our Saint was "a very pillar of religion, . . . a most steadfast defender of justice and truth" (*ibid.*, I, 1, p. 54), her biographer says. By her words and example she kindled great fervor in other people. To the prayers and penances of the monastic Rule she added others with such devotion and such trusting abandonment in God that she inspired in those who met her an awareness of being in the Lord's presence. In fact, God made her understand that he had called her to be an instrument of his grace. Gertrude herself felt unworthy of this immense divine treasure and confesses that she had not safeguarded it or made enough of it. She exclaimed: "If you had given me, in my unworthiness, no more than a thread of flax as a memento, I should have respected it and treated it more reverently [I did than your gifts]" (*ibid.*, II, 5, p. 103). Yet, in recognizing her poverty and worthlessness, she adhered to God's will, "because", she said,

> I consider that I have profited but little from your gifts, and so I cannot believe that they were meant for me alone, because in your eternal wisdom you cannot be misled. That is why, Giver of gifts, you who have so freely loaded me with gifts unmerited, I ask you to grant that at least one loving heart reading these pages may be moved to compassion, seeing that through zeal for souls you have permitted such a royal gem to be embedded in the slime of my heart. (*Ibid.*)

Two favors in particular were dearer to her than any other, as Gertrude herself writes:

> They are the seal put on my heart . . . with those brilliant jewels which are your salvific wounds, and the wound of love with which you so manifestly and efficaciously transfixed my heart. Had you given me no other consolation, interior or exterior, these two gifts alone would have held so much happiness that, were I to live a thousand years, I could never exhaust the fund of consolation, learning, and feelings of gratitude that I should derive from them at each hour. In addition to all these favors, you have granted me the priceless gift of your familiar friendship, giving me in various ways, to my indescribable delight, the noblest treasure of the divinity, your divine heart. . . . To all these other benefits you have added a crowning one in giving me your dearest mother, the most blessed Virgin Mary, to take care of me, commending me to her affection as often as a

bridegroom commends his dearly beloved bride to his own mother. (*Ibid.*, II, 23, pp. 130–31.)

Looking forward to never-ending communion, she ended her earthly life on 17 November 1301 or 1302, at the age of about forty-six. In the seventh Exercise, that of preparation for death, Saint Gertrude wrote: "O Jesus, you who are immensely dear to me, be with me always, so that my heart may stay with you and that your love may endure with me with no possibility of division; and bless my passing, so that my spirit, freed from the bonds of the flesh, may immediately find rest in you. Amen" (*Spiritual Exercises*, Milan, 2006, p. 148).

It seems obvious to me that these are not only things of the past, of history; rather Saint Gertrude's life lives on as a lesson of Christian life, of an upright path, and shows us that the heart of a happy life, of a true life, is friendship with the Lord Jesus. And this friendship is learned in love for Sacred Scripture, in love for the liturgy, in profound faith, in love for Mary, so as to be ever more truly acquainted with God himself and hence with true happiness, which is the goal of our life.

18

Blessed Angela of Foligno

WEDNESDAY, 13 OCTOBER 2010
Saint Peter's Square

Dear Brothers and Sisters,

Today I would like to speak to you about Blessed Angela of Foligno, a great medieval mystic who lived in the thirteenth century. People are usually fascinated by the consummate experience of union with God that she reached, but perhaps they give too little consideration to her first steps, her conversion, and the long journey that led from her starting point, the "great fear of hell", to her goal, total union with the Trinity. The first part of Angela's life was certainly not that of a fervent disciple of the Lord. She was born into a well-off family in about 1248. Her father died, and she was brought up in a somewhat superficial manner by her mother. She was introduced at a rather young age into the worldly circles of the town of Foligno, where she met a man whom she married at the age of twenty and to whom she bore children. Her life was so carefree that she was even contemptuous of the so-called "penitents", who abounded in that period; they were people who, in order to follow Christ, sold their possessions and lived in prayer, fasting, in service to the Church, and in charity.

Certain events, such as the violent earthquake in 1279, a hurricane, the endless war against Perugia, and its harsh consequences, affected the life of Angela, who little by little became aware of her sins, until she took a decisive step. In 1285 she called upon Saint Francis, who appeared to her in a vision, and asked his advice on making a good general confession. She then went to confession with a friar in San Feliciano. Three years later, on her path of conversion she reached another turning point: she was released from any emotional ties. In the space of a few months, her mother's death was followed by the death of her husband and those of all her children. She therefore sold her possessions and in 1291 enrolled in the Third Order of Saint Francis. She died in Foligno on 4 January 1309.

The Book of Visions and Instructions of Blessed Angela of Foligno, in which is gathered the documentation on our Blessed, tells the story of this conversion and points out the necessary means: penance, humility, and tribulation; and it recounts the steps, Angela's successive experiences, which began in 1285. Remembering them after she had experienced them, Angela then endeavored to recount them through her friar confessor, who faithfully transcribed them, seeking later to sort them into stages which he called "steps or mutations" but without managing to put them entirely in order (cf. *Il Libro della beata Angela da Foligno*, Cinisello Balsamo, 1990, p. 51). This was because for Blessed Angela the experience of union meant the total involvement of both the spiritual and physical senses, and she was left with only a "shadow" in her mind, as it were, of what she had "understood" during her ecstasies. "I truly heard these words", she confessed after a mystical ecstasy, "but it is in no way possible for me to know or tell of what I saw and understood, or of what he [God] showed me, although I would willingly reveal what I understood with the words that I heard, but it was an absolutely ineffable abyss." Angela of Foligno presented her mystical "life" without elaborating on it herself because these were divine illuminations that were communicated suddenly and unexpectedly to her soul. Her friar confessor, too, had difficulty in reporting these events, "partly because of her great and wonderful reserve concerning the divine gifts" (*ibid.*, p. 194). In addition to Angela's difficulty in expressing her mystical experience was the difficulty her listeners found in understanding her. It was a situation which showed clearly that the one true Teacher, Jesus, dwells in the heart of every believer and wants to take total possession of it. So it was with Angela, who wrote to a spiritual son: "My son, if you were to see my heart, you would be absolutely obliged to do everything God wants, because my heart is God's heart and God's heart is mine." Here Saint Paul's words ring out: "It is no longer I who live, but Christ who lives in me" (Gal 2:20).

Let us then consider only a few "steps" of our Blessed's rich spiritual journey. The first, in fact, is an introduction: "It was the knowledge of sin," as she explained, "after which my soul was deeply afraid of damnation; in this stage I shed bitter tears" (*Il Libro della beata Angela da Foligno*, p. 39). This "dread" of hell corresponds to the type of faith that Angela had at the time of her "conversion"; it was a faith still poor in charity, that is, in love of God. Repentance, the fear of hell, and penance unfolded to Angela the prospect of the sorrowful "Way of the Cross", which from the eighth to the fifteenth stages was to lead her to the "way of love". Her friar confessor recounted: "The faithful woman then told me: I have had this divine revelation: 'After the things you have written, write that anyone who wishes to preserve grace must not lift the eyes of his soul from the

Cross, either in the joy or in the sadness that I grant or permit him'" (*ibid.*, p. 143). However, in this phase Angela "did not yet feel love". She said: "The soul feels shame and bitterness and does not yet feel love but suffering" (*ibid.*, p. 39) and is not satisfied.

Angela felt she should give something to God in reparation for her sins but slowly came to realize that she had nothing to give him, indeed, that she "was nothing" before him. She understood that it would not be her will that would give her God's love, for her will could give only her own "nothingness", her "non-love". As she was to say: only "true and pure love, which comes from God, is in the soul and ensures that one recognizes one's own shortcomings and the divine goodness. . . . Such love brings the soul to Christ, and it understands with certainty that in him no deception can be found or can exist. No particle of worldly love can be mingled with this love" (*ibid.*, pp. 124–25). This meant opening herself solely and totally to God's love, whose greatest expression is in Christ: "O my God," she prayed, "make me worthy of knowing the loftiest mystery that your most ardent and ineffable love brought about for our sake, together with the love of the Trinity, in other words, the loftiest mystery of your most holy Incarnation. . . . O incomprehensible love! There is no greater love than this love that brought my God to become man in order to make me God" (*ibid.*, p. 295). However, Angela's heart always bore the wounds of sin; even after a good confession, she would find herself forgiven and yet still stricken by sin, free and yet conditioned by the past, absolved but in need of penance. And the thought of hell accompanied her, too, for the greater the progress the soul makes on the way of Christian perfection, the more convinced it is not only of being "unworthy" but also of deserving of hell.

And so it was that on this mystical journey Angela understood the central reality in a profound way: what would save her from her "unworthiness" and from "deserving hell" would not be her "union with God" or her possession of the "truth", but Jesus Crucified, "his crucifixion for me", his love. In the eighth step, she said, "However, I did not yet understand whether the greater good was my liberation from sins and from hell and conversion to penance or his Crucifixion for me" (*ibid.*, p. 41). This was the precarious balance between love and suffering that she felt throughout her arduous journey toward perfection. For this very reason, she preferred to contemplate Christ Crucified, because in this vision she saw the perfect balance brought about. On the Cross was the man-God, in a supreme act of suffering which was a supreme act of love. In the third *Instruction*, the Blessed insisted on this contemplation and declared: "The more perfectly and purely we see, the more perfectly and purely we love. . . . Therefore the more we see the God and man Jesus Christ, the more we are transformed in him through love. . . . What I said of love . . . I also say of suffering: the more the soul contemplates the ineffable suffering of the God and man Jesus Christ, the more sorrowful it becomes and is transformed through suffering" (*ibid.*, pp. 190–91). Thus, uniting herself with and transforming herself into the love and suffering of Christ Crucified, she was identifying herself with him. Angela's conversion, which began from that confession in 1285, was to reach maturity only when God's forgiveness appeared to her soul as the freely given gift of the love of the Father, the source of love: "No one can make excuses," she said, "because anyone can love God, and he does not ask the soul for more than to love him, because he loves the soul, and it is his love" (*ibid.*, p. 76).

On Angela's spiritual journey, the transition from conversion to mystical experience, from what can be expressed to the inexpressible, took place through the Crucified One. He is the "God-man of the Passion" who became her "teacher of perfection". The whole of her mystical experience, therefore, consisted in striving for a perfect "likeness" with him, through ever deeper and ever more radical purifications and transformations. Angela threw her whole self, body and soul, into this stupendous undertaking, never sparing herself penance and suffering, from beginning to end, desiring to die with all the sorrows suffered by the God-man crucified in order to be totally transformed in him. "O children of God," she recommended, "transform yourselves totally in the man-God, who so loved you that he chose to die for you a most ignominious and altogether unutterably painful death, and in the most painful and bitterest way. And this was solely for love of you, O man!" (*ibid.*, p. 247). This identification also meant experiencing what Jesus himself experienced: poverty, contempt, and sorrow, because, as she declared, "through temporal poverty the soul will find eternal riches; through contempt and shame it will obtain supreme honor and very great glory; through a little penance, made with pain and sorrow, it will possess with infinite sweetness and consolation the Supreme Good, Eternal God" (*ibid.*, p. 293).

From conversion to mystic union with Christ Crucified to the inexpressible. A very lofty journey, whose secret is constant prayer. "The more you pray," she said,

> the more illumined you will be and the more profoundly and intensely you will see the supreme Good, the supremely good Being; the more profoundly and intensely you see him, the more you will love him; the more you love him, the more he will delight you; and the more he delights

> you, the better you will understand him, and you will become capable of understanding him. You will then reach the fullness of light, for you will understand that you cannot understand. (*Ibid.*, p. 184.)

Dear brothers and sisters, Blessed Angela's life began with a worldly existence, rather remote from God. Yet her meeting with the figure of Saint Francis and, finally, her meeting with Christ Crucified reawakened her soul to the presence of God, for the reason that with God alone life becomes true life, because, in sorrow for sin, it becomes love and joy. And this is how Blessed Angela speaks to us. Today we all risk living as though God did not exist; he seems so distant from daily life. However, God has thousands of ways of his own for each one, to make himself present in the soul, to show that he exists and knows and loves me. And Blessed Angela wishes to make us attentive to these signs with which the Lord touches our soul, attentive to God's presence, so as to learn the way with God and toward God, in communion with Christ Crucified. Let us pray the Lord that he make us attentive to the signs of his presence and that he teach us truly to live.

19

Saint Elizabeth of Hungary

WEDNESDAY, 20 OCTOBER 2010

Saint Peter's Square

Dear Brothers and Sisters,

Today I would like to speak to you about one of the women of the Middle Ages who inspired the greatest admiration; she is Saint Elizabeth of Hungary, also called Saint Elizabeth of Thuringia.

Elizabeth was born in 1207; historians dispute her birthplace. Her father was Andrew II, the rich and powerful King of Hungary. To reinforce political ties, he had married the German Countess Gertrude of Andechs-Meran, sister of Saint Hedwig, who was wife to the Duke of Silesia. Elizabeth, together with her sister and three brothers, spent only the first four years of her childhood at the Hungarian court. She liked playing, music, and dancing; she recited her prayers faithfully and already showed special attention to the poor, whom she helped with a kind word or an affectionate gesture.

Her happy childhood was suddenly interrupted when some knights arrived from distant Thuringia to escort her to her new residence in Central Germany. In fact, complying with the customs of that time, Elizabeth's father had arranged for her to become a Princess of Thuringia. The Landgrave or Count of this region was one of the richest and most influential sovereigns in Europe at the beginning of the thirteenth century, and his castle was a center of magnificence and culture. However, the festivities and apparent glory concealed the ambition of feudal princes, who were frequently warring with each other and in conflict with the royal and imperial authorities. In this context, the Landgrave Hermann very willingly accepted the betrothal of his son Ludwig to the Hungarian Princess. Elizabeth left her homeland with a rich dowry and a large entourage, including her personal ladies-in-waiting, two of whom were to remain faithful friends to the very end. It is they who left us the precious information on the childhood and life of the Saint.

They reached Eisenach after a long journey and made the ascent to the Fortress of Wartburg, the strong castle towering over the city. It was here that the betrothal of Ludwig and Elizabeth was celebrated. In the ensuing years, while Ludwig learned the knightly profession, Elizabeth and her companions studied German, French, Latin, music, literature, and embroidery. Despite the fact that political reasons had determined their betrothal, a sincere love developed between the two young people, enlivened by faith and by the desire to do God's will. On his father's death, when Ludwig was eighteen years old, he began to reign over Thuringia. Elizabeth, however, became the object of critical whispers because her behavior was incongruous with court life. Hence their marriage celebrations were far from sumptuous, and a part of the funds destined for the banquet was donated to the poor. With her profound sensitivity, Elizabeth saw the contradictions between the faith professed and Christian practice. She could not bear compromise. Once, on entering a church on the Feast of the Assumption, she took off her crown, laid it before the

Crucifix, and, covering her face, lay prostrate on the ground. When her mother-in-law reprimanded her for this gesture, Elizabeth answered: "How can I, a wretched creature, continue to wear a crown of earthly dignity when I see my King Jesus Christ crowned with thorns?" She behaved to her subjects in the same way that she behaved to God. Among the *Sayings of the Four Maids* we find this testimony: "She did not eat any food before ascertaining that it came from her husband's property or legitimate possessions. While she abstained from goods procured illegally, she also did her utmost to provide compensation to those who had suffered violence" (nos. 25 and 37). She is a true example for all who have roles of leadership: the exercise of authority, at every level, must be lived as a service to justice and charity, in the constant search for the common good.

Elizabeth diligently practiced works of mercy: she would give food and drink to those who knocked at her door; she procured clothing, paid debts, cared for the sick, and buried the dead. Coming down from her castle, she often visited the homes of the poor with her ladies-in-waiting, bringing them bread, meat, flour, and other food. She distributed the food personally and attentively checked the clothing and mattresses of the poor. This behavior was reported to her husband, who not only was not displeased but answered her accusers, "So long as she does not sell the castle, I am happy with her!" The miracle of the loaves that were changed into roses fits into this context: while Elizabeth was on her way with her apron filled with bread for the poor, she met her husband, who asked her what she was carrying. She opened her apron to show him, and, instead of bread, it was full of magnificent roses. This symbol of charity often features in depictions of Saint Elizabeth.

Elizabeth's marriage was profoundly happy: she helped her husband to raise his human qualities to a supernatural level, and he, in exchange, stood up for his wife's generosity to the poor and for her religious practices. In ever greater admiration of his wife's great faith, Ludwig said to her, referring to her attention to the poor: "Dear Elizabeth, it is Christ whom you have cleansed, nourished, and cared for." A clear witness to how faith and love of God and neighbor strengthen family life and deepen ever more the matrimonial union.

The young couple found spiritual support in the Friars Minor, who began to spread through Thuringia in 1222. Elizabeth chose from among them Friar Rodeger (Rüdiger) as her spiritual director. When he told her about the event of the conversion of Francis of Assisi, a rich young merchant, Elizabeth was even more enthusiastic in the journey of her Christian life. From that time she became even more determined to follow the poor and Crucified Christ, present in poor people. Even when her first son was born, followed by two other children, our Saint never neglected her charitable works. She also helped the Friars Minor to build a convent at Halberstadt, of which Friar Rodeger became superior. For this reason Elizabeth's spiritual direction was taken on by Conrad of Marburg.

The farewell to her husband was a hard trial, when, at the end of June in 1227, Ludwig IV joined the Crusade of the Emperor Frederick II. He reminded his wife that this was traditional for the sovereigns of Thuringia. Elizabeth answered him: "Far be it from me to detain you. I have given my whole self to God, and now I must also give you." However, fever decimated the troops, and Ludwig himself fell ill and died in Otranto, before embarking, in September 1227. He was twenty-seven years old. When

Elizabeth learned the news, she was so sorrowful that she withdrew in solitude; but then, strengthened by prayer and comforted by the hope of seeing him again in Heaven, she began to attend to the affairs of the Kingdom. However, another trial was lying in wait for Elizabeth. Her brother-in-law usurped the government of Thuringia, declaring himself to be the true heir of Ludwig and accusing Elizabeth of being a pious woman incapable of ruling. The young widow, with three children, was banished from the Castle of Wartburg and went in search of a place of refuge. Only two of her ladies remained close to her. They accompanied her and entrusted the three children to the care of Ludwig's friends. Wandering through the villages, Elizabeth worked wherever she was welcomed, looked after the sick, spun thread, and cooked. During this calvary, which she bore with great faith, with patience, and with dedication to God, a few relatives who had stayed faithful to her and viewed her brother-in-law's rule as illegal, restored her reputation. So it was that, at the beginning of 1228, Elizabeth received sufficient income to withdraw to the family's castle in Marburg, where her spiritual director, Conrad, also lived. It was he who reported the following event to Pope Gregory IX:

> On Good Friday in 1228, having placed her hands on the altar in the chapel of her city, Eisenach, to which she had welcomed the Friars Minor, in the presence of several friars and relatives, Elizabeth renounced her own will and all the vanities of the world. She also wanted to resign all her possessions, but I dissuaded her out of love for the poor. Shortly afterward she built a hospital, gathered the sick and invalids, and served at her own table the most wretched and deprived. When I reprimanded her for these things, Elizabeth answered that she received from the poor special grace and humility. (*Epistula magistri Conradi*, 14–17.)

We can discern in this affirmation a certain mystical experience similar to that of Saint Francis: the *Poverello* of Assisi declared in his testament, in fact, that serving lepers, which he at first found repugnant, was transformed into sweetness of the soul and of the body (*Testamentum*, 1–3). Elizabeth spent her last three years in the hospital she founded, serving the sick and keeping vigil with the dying. She always tried to carry out the most humble services and repugnant tasks. She became what we might call a consecrated woman in the world (*soror in saeculo*) and, with other friends clothed in grey habits, formed a religious community. It is not by chance that she is the Patroness of the Third Order Regular of Saint Francis and of the Franciscan Secular Order.

In November 1231 she was stricken with a high fever. When the news of her illness spread, many people flocked to see her. After about ten days, she asked for the doors to be closed so that she might be alone with God. In the night of 17 November, she fell asleep gently in the Lord. The testimonies of her holiness were so many and such that after only four years Pope Gregory IX canonized her, and, that same year, the beautiful church built in her honor at Marburg was consecrated.

Dear brothers and sisters, in Saint Elizabeth we see how faith and friendship with Christ create a sense of justice, of the equality of all, of the rights of others, and how they create love, charity. And from this charity is born hope, too, the certainty that we are loved by Christ and that the love of Christ awaits us, thereby rendering us capable of imitating Christ and of seeing Christ in others. Saint Elizabeth invites us to rediscover Christ, to love him, and to have faith, and, thereby, to find true justice and love, as well as the joy that one day we shall be immersed in divine love, in the joy of eternity with God.

20

Saint Bridget of Sweden

WEDNESDAY, 27 OCTOBER 2010

Saint Peter's Square

Dear Brothers and Sisters,

On the eve of the Great Jubilee in anticipation of the Year 2000, the Venerable Servant of God John Paul II proclaimed Saint Bridget of Sweden Co-Patroness of the whole of Europe. This morning I would like to present her, her message, and the reasons why—still today—this holy woman has much to teach the Church and the world.

We are well acquainted with the events of Saint Bridget's life because her spiritual fathers compiled her biography in order to further the process of her canonization immediately after her death in 1373. Bridget had been born seventy years earlier, in 1303, in Finster, Sweden, a Northern European nation that for three centuries had welcomed the Christian faith with the same enthusiasm as that with which the Saint had received it from her parents, very devout people who belonged to noble families closely related to the reigning house.

We can distinguished *two periods* in this Saint's life.

The *first* was characterized by her happily married state. Her husband was called Ulf, and he was Governor of an important district of the Kingdom of Sweden. The marriage lasted for twenty-eight years, until Ulf's death. Eight children were born, the second of whom, Karin (Catherine), is venerated as a Saint. This is an eloquent sign of Bridget's dedication to her children's education. Moreover, King Magnus of Sweden so appreciated her pedagogical wisdom that he summoned her to court for a time, so that she could introduce his young wife, Blanche of Namur, to Swedish culture. Bridget, who was given spiritual guidance by a learned religious who initiated her into the study of the Scriptures, exercised a very positive influence on her family, which, thanks to her presence, became a true "domestic church". Together with her husband she adopted the Rule of the Franciscan Tertiaries. She generously practiced works of charity for the poor; she also founded a hospital. At his wife's side, Ulf's character improved, and he advanced in the Christian life. On their return from a long pilgrimage to Santiago de Compostela, which they made in 1341 with other members of the family, the couple developed a project of living in continence; but a little while later, in the tranquility of a monastery to which he had retired, Ulf's earthly life ended. This first period of Bridget's life helps us to appreciate what today we could describe as an authentic "conjugal spirituality": together, Christian spouses can make a journey of holiness sustained by the grace of the sacrament of Marriage. It is often the woman, as happened in the life of Saint Bridget and Ulf, who with her religious sensitivity, delicacy, and gentleness succeeds in persuading her husband to follow a path of faith. I am thinking with gratitude of the many women who, day after day, illuminate their families with their witness of Christian life in our time, too. May the Lord's Spirit still inspire holiness in Christian spouses today, to show the world the beauty of marriage lived in accordance with the Gospel values: love, tenderness, reciprocal help, fruitfulness in begetting and in raising children, openness and solidarity to the world, and participation in the life of the Church.

The *second* period of Bridget's life began when she was widowed. She did not consider another marriage in order to deepen her union with the Lord through prayer, penance, and charitable works. Therefore Christian widows, too, may find in this Saint a model to follow. In fact, upon the death of her husband, after distributing her possessions to the poor—although she never became a consecrated religious—Bridget settled near the Cistercian Monastery of Alvastra. Here began the divine revelations that were to accompany her for the rest of her life. Bridget dictated them to her confessors-secretaries, who translated them from Swedish into Latin and gathered them in eight volumes entitled *Revelationes* (Revelations). A supplement followed these books called, precisely, *Revelationes extravagantes* (Supplementary revelations).

Saint Bridget's *Revelations* have a very varied content and style. At times the revelations are presented in the form of dialogues between the Divine Persons, the Virgin, the saints, and even demons; they are dialogues in which Bridget also takes part. At other times, instead, a specific vision is described; and in yet others, what the Virgin Mary reveals to her concerning the life and mysteries of the Son. The value of Saint Bridget's *Revelations*, sometimes the object of criticism, Venerable John Paul II explained in his Letter *Spes Aedificandi*: "The Church, which recognized Bridget's holiness without ever pronouncing on her individual revelations, has accepted the overall authenticity of her interior experience" (no. 5). Indeed, reading these *Revelations* challenges us on many important topics. For example, the description of Christ's Passion, with very realistic details, frequently recurs. Bridget always had a special devotion to Christ's Passion, contemplating in it God's infinite love for man. She boldly places these words on the lips of the Lord, who speaks to her: "O my friends, I love my sheep so tenderly that were it possible I would die many other times for each one of them that same death I suffered for the redemption of all" (*Revelationes* I, 59). The sorrowful motherhood of Mary, which made her Mediatrix and Mother of Mercy, is also a subject that recurs frequently in the *Revelations*.

In receiving these charisms, Bridget was aware that she had been given a gift of special love on the Lord's part: "My Daughter"—we read in the first book of *Revelations*—"I have chosen you for myself, love me with all your heart . . . more than all that exists in the world" (chap. 1). Bridget, moreover, knew well and was firmly convinced that every charism is destined to build up the Church. For this very reason many of her revelations were addressed in the form of admonishments, even severe ones, to the believers of her time, including the religious and political authorities, that they might live a consistent Christian life; but she always reprimanded them with an attitude of respect and of full fidelity to the Magisterium of the Church and in particular to the Successor of the Apostle Peter.

In 1349 Bridget left Sweden for good and went on pilgrimage to Rome. She was not only intending to take part in the Jubilee of the Year 1350 but also wished to obtain from the Pope approval for the Rule of a religious order that she was intending to found, called after the Holy Savior and made up of monks and nuns under the authority of the abbess. This is an element we should not find surprising: in the Middle Ages monastic foundations existed with both male and female branches, but with the practice of the same monastic rule that provided for the abbess' direction.

In fact, in the great Christian tradition, the woman is accorded special dignity and—always based on the example of Mary, Queen of Apostles—a place of her own in the Church, which, without coinciding with the ordained priesthood, is equally important for the spiritual growth of the Community. Furthermore, the collaboration of consecrated men and women, always with respect for their specific vocation, is of great importance in the contemporary world. In Rome, in the company of her daughter Karin, Bridget dedicated herself to a life of intense apostolate and prayer. And from Rome she went on pilgrimage to various Italian Shrines, in particular to Assisi, the homeland of Saint Francis, for whom Bridget had always had great devotion. Finally, in 1371, her deepest desire was crowned: to travel to the Holy Land, to which she went accompanied by her spiritual children, a group that Bridget called "the friends of God". In those years the Pontiffs lived at Avignon, a long way from Rome: Bridget addressed a heartfelt plea to them to return to the See of Peter, in the Eternal City. She died in 1373, before Pope Gregory XI returned to Rome definitively. She was buried temporarily in the Church of San Lorenzo in Panisperna in Rome, but in 1374 her children Birger and Karin took her body back to her homeland, to the Monastery of Vadstena, the headquarters of the Religious Order Saint Bridget had founded. The Order immediately experienced a considerable expansion. In 1391, Pope Boniface IX solemnly canonized her. Bridget's holiness, characterized by the multiplicity of her gifts and the experiences that I have wished to recall in this brief biographical and spiritual outline, makes her an eminent figure in European history. In coming from Scandinavia, Saint Bridget bears witness to the way Christianity had deeply permeated the life of all the peoples of this Continent. In declaring her Co-Patroness of Europe, Pope John Paul II hoped that Saint Bridget—who lived in the fourteenth century, when Western Christianity had not yet been wounded by division—might intercede effectively with God to obtain the grace of full Christian unity so deeply longed for. Let us pray, dear brothers and sisters, for this same intention, which we have very much at heart, and that Europe might always be nourished by its Christian roots, invoking the powerful intercession of Saint Bridget of Sweden, a faithful disciple of God and Co-Patroness of Europe.

21

Marguerite d'Oingt

WEDNESDAY, 3 NOVEMBER 2010
Paul VI Hall

Dear Brothers and Sisters,

With Marguerite d'Oingt, of whom I would like to speak to you today, we are introduced to Carthusian spirituality, which draws its inspiration from the evangelical synthesis lived and proposed by Saint Bruno. We do not know the date of her birth, although some place it around 1240. Marguerite came from a powerful family of the old nobility of Lyons, the Oingt. We know that her mother was also called Marguerite and that she had two brothers—Giscard and Louis—and three sisters: Catherine, Elizabeth, and Agnes. The latter followed her to the Carthusian monastery, succeeding her as Prioress.

We have no information on her childhood, but from her writings it seems that she spent it peacefully in an affectionate family environment. In fact, to express God's boundless love, she valued images linked to the family, with particular reference to the figure of the father and of the mother. In one of her meditations she prays thus: "Most gentle Lord, when I think of the special graces that you have given me through your solicitude: first of all, how you took care of me since my childhood and how you removed me from the danger of this world and called me to dedicate myself to your holy service, and how you provided everything that was necessary for me: food, drink, dress, and footwear (and you did so) in such a way that I had no occasion in these things to think of anything but your great mercy" (Marguerite d'Oingt, *Scritti Spirituali, Meditazione* V, 100, Cinisello Balsamo, 1997, p. 74).

Again from her meditations we know that she entered the Carthusian monastery of Poleteins in response to the Lord's call, leaving everything behind and accepting the strict Carthusian Rule in order to belong totally to the Lord, to be with him always. She wrote:

> Gentle Lord, I left my father and my mother and my siblings and all the things of this world for love of you; but this is very little, because the riches of this world are but thorns that prick; and the more one possesses, the more unfortunate one is. And because of this it seems to me that I left nothing other than misery and poverty; but you know, gentle Lord, that if I possessed a thousand worlds and could dispose of them as I pleased, I would abandon everything for love of you; and even if you gave me everything that you possess in Heaven and on earth, I would not feel satisfied until I had you, because you are the life of my soul; I do not have and do not want to have a father and mother outside of you. (*Ibid., Meditazione* II, 32, p. 59.)

We also have little data on her life in the Carthusian monastery. We know that in 1288 she became its fourth Prioress, a post she held until her death, 11 February 1310. From her writings, however, we do not deduce particular stages in her spiritual itinerary. She conceived the entirety of life as a journey of purification up to full configuration with Christ. He is the book that is written, which is inscribed daily in her own heart and life, in particular his saving Passion. In the work *Speculum*, referring to herself in the third person, Marguerite stresses that by the Lord's grace "she had engraved in her heart the holy life that Jesus Christ, God, led on earth, his good example and his good doctrine. She had placed the gentle Jesus Christ so well in her heart that it even seemed to her that he was present and that he had a closed book in his hand, to instruct her" (*ibid.*, I, 2–3, p. 81). "In this book she found written the life that Jesus Christ led on earth, from his birth to his ascension into Heaven" (*ibid.*, I, 12, p. 83). Every day, beginning in the morning, Marguerite dedicated herself to the study of this book. And, when she had looked at it well, she began to read the book of her own conscience, which showed the falsehoods and lies of her own life (cf. *ibid.*, I, 6–7, p. 82); she wrote about herself to help others and to fix more deeply in her heart the grace of the presence of God, so as to make every day of her life marked by comparison with the words and actions of Jesus, with the Book of his life. And she did this so that Christ's life would be imprinted in her soul in a permanent and profound way, until she was able to see the Book internally, that is, until she could contemplate the mystery of the triune God (cf. *ibid.*, II, 14–22; III, 23–40, pp. 84–90).

Through her writings, Marguerite gives us some traces of her spirituality, enabling us to understand some features of her personality and of her gifts of governance. She was a very learned woman; she usually wrote in Latin, the language of the erudite, but she also wrote in Provençal, and this too is a rarity: thus her writings are the first of those known to be written in that language. She lived a life rich in mystical experiences described with simplicity, allowing one to intuit the ineffable mystery of God, stressing the limits of the mind to apprehend it and the inadequacy of human language to express it. Marguerite had a linear personality, simple, open, of gentle affectivity, great balance, and acute discernment, able to enter into the depths of the human spirit, discerning its limits, its ambiguities, but also its aspirations, the soul's *élan* toward God. She showed an outstanding aptitude for governance, combining her profound mystical spiritual life with service to her sisters and to the community. Significant in this connection is a passage of a letter to her father. She wrote: "My dear father, I wish to inform you that I am very busy because of the needs of our house, so that I am unable to apply my mind to good thoughts; in fact, I have so much to do that I do not know which way to turn. We did not harvest the wheat in the seventh month of the year, and our vineyards were destroyed by the storm. Moreover, our church is in such a sorry state that we are obliged to reconstruct it in part" (*ibid.*, *Lettere*, III, 14, p. 127).

A Carthusian nun describes the figure of Marguerite in this way: "Revealed through her work is a fascinating personality, of lively intelligence, oriented to speculation and at the same time favored by mystical graces: in a word, a holy and wise woman who is able to express with a certain humor an affectivity altogether spiritual" (*Una Monaca Certosina*; *Certosine*, in the *Dizionario degli Istituti di Perfezione*, Rome, 1975, col. 777). In the dynamism of mystical life, Marguerite valued the experience of natural affections, purified by grace, as a privileged means to understand more profoundly and to second divine action with greater alacrity and ardor. The reason lies in the fact that man is created in the image of God and is therefore called to build with God a wonderful history of love, allowing himself to be totally involved in his initiative.

The triune God, the God who is love and who reveals himself in Christ, fascinated her, and Marguerite lived a relationship of profound love for the Lord. In contrast, she sees human ingratitude to the point of betrayal, even to the paradox of the Cross. She says that the Cross of Christ is similar to the table of childbirth. Jesus' pain is compared with that of a mother. She wrote:

> The mother who carried me in her womb suffered greatly in giving birth to me, for a day or a night, but you, most gentle Lord, were tormented for me not only for one night or one day, but for more than thirty years! . . . How bitterly you suffered because of me throughout your life! And when the moment of delivery arrived, your work was so painful that your holy sweat became as drops of blood which ran down your whole body to the ground. (*Ibid.*, *Meditazione* I, 33, p. 59.)

In evoking the accounts of Jesus' Passion, Marguerite contemplated these sorrows with profound compassion. She said:

> You were placed on the hard bed of the Cross, so that you could not move or turn or shake your limbs as a man usually does when suffering great pain, because you were completely stretched and pierced with the nails . . . and . . . all your muscles and veins were lacerated. . . . But all these pains . . . were still not sufficient for you, so much so that you desired that your side be pierced so cruelly by the lance that your defenseless body should be totally plowed and torn and your precious blood spurted with such violence that it formed a long path, almost as if it were a current.

Referring to Mary, she said: "It was no wonder that the sword that lacerated your body also penetrated the heart of your glorious Mother, who so wanted to support you, . . .

because your love was loftier than any other love" (*ibid.*, *Meditazione* II, 36–39, 42, pp. 60f.).

Dear friends, Marguerite d'Oingt invites us to meditate daily on the life of sorrow and love of Jesus and that of his Mother, Mary. Here is our hope, the meaning of our existence. From contemplation of Christ's love for us are born the strength and joy to respond with the same love, placing our life at the service of God and of others. With Marguerite we also say: "Gentle Lord, all that you did, for love of me and of the whole human race, leads me to love you, but the remembrance of your most holy Passion gives unequalled vigor to my power of affection to love you. That is why it seems to me that . . . I have found what I so much desired: not to love anything other than you or in you or for love of you" (*ibid.*, *Meditazione* II, 46, p. 62).

At first glance this figure of a Medieval Carthusian nun, as well as her life and her thought, seems distant from us, from our life, from our way of thinking and acting. But if we look at what is essential in this life, we see that it also affects us and that it should also become essential in our own existence.

We have heard that Marguerite considered the Lord as a book; she fixed her gaze on the Lord; she considered him a mirror in which her own conscience also appeared. And from this mirror, light entered her soul. She let into her own being the word, the life of Christ, and thus she was transformed; her conscience was enlightened; she found criteria and light and was cleansed. It is precisely this that we also need: to let the words, life, and light of Christ enter our conscience so that it is enlightened, understands what is true and good and what is wrong; may our conscience be enlightened and cleansed. Rubbish is not only on some streets of the world. There is also rubbish in our consciences and in our souls. Only the light of the Lord, his strength and his love, cleanses us, purifies us, showing us the right path. Therefore, let us follow holy Marguerite in this gaze fixed on Jesus. Let us read the book of his life; let us allow ourselves to be enlightened and cleansed, to learn the true life.

22

Saint Juliana of Cornillon

WEDNESDAY, 17 NOVEMBER 2010

Dear Brothers and Sisters,

This morning, too, I would like to introduce a female figure to you. She is little known, but the Church is deeply indebted to her, not only because of the holiness of her life but also because, with her great fervor, she contributed to the institution of one of the most important solemn liturgies of the year: *Corpus Christi*. She is Saint Juliana de Cornillon, also known as Saint Juliana of Liège. We know several facts about her life, mainly from a biography that was probably written by a contemporary cleric; it is a collection of various testimonies of people who were directly acquainted with the Saint.

Juliana was born near Liège, Belgium, between 1191 and 1192. It is important to emphasize this place because at that time the Diocese of Liège was, so to speak, a true "Eucharistic Upper Room". Before Juliana, eminent theologians had illustrated the supreme value of the sacrament of the Eucharist, and, again in Liège, there were groups of women generously dedicated to Eucharistic worship and to fervent Communion. Guided by exemplary priests, they lived together, devoting themselves to prayer and to charitable works.

Orphaned at the age of five, Juliana, together with her sister Agnes, was entrusted to the care of the Augustinian nuns at the convent and leprosarium of Mont-Cornillon. She was taught mainly by a sister called "Sapienza" [wisdom], who was in charge of her spiritual development to the time Juliana received the religious habit and thus became an Augustinian nun. She became so learned that she could read the words of the Church Fathers, of Saint Augustine and Saint Bernard in particular, in Latin. In addition to a keen intelligence, Juliana showed a special propensity for contemplation from the outset. She had a profound sense of Christ's presence, which she experienced by living the sacrament of the Eucharist with special intensity and by pausing frequently to meditate upon Jesus' words: "And lo, I am with you always, to the close of the age" (Mt 28:20).

When Juliana was sixteen, she had her first vision, which recurred subsequently several times during her Eucharistic adoration. Her vision presented the moon in its full splendor, crossed diametrically by a dark stripe. The Lord made her understand the meaning of what had appeared to her. The moon symbolized the life of the Church on earth, the opaque line, on the other hand, represented the absence of a liturgical feast for whose institution Juliana was asked to plead effectively: namely, a feast in which believers would be able to adore the Eucharist so as to increase in faith, to advance in the practice of the virtues, and to make reparation for offenses to the Most Holy Sacrament.

Juliana, who in the meantime had become Prioress of the convent, for twenty years kept secret this revelation that had filled her heart with joy. She then confided it to two other fervent adorers of the Eucharist, Blessed Eva, who lived as a hermit, and Isabella, who had joined her at the Monastery of Mont-Cornillon.

The three women established a sort of "spiritual alliance" for the purpose of glorifying the Most Holy Sacrament. They also chose to involve a highly regarded priest, John of Lausanne, who was a canon of the Church of Saint Martin in Liège. They asked him to consult theologians and clerics on what was important to them. Their affirmative response was encouraging.

What happened to Juliana of Cornillon occurs frequently in the lives of Saints. To have confirmation that an inspiration comes from God, it is always necessary to be immersed in prayer, to wait patiently, to seek friendship and exchanges with other good souls, and to submit all things to the judgment of the Pastors of the Church. It was in fact the Bishop of Liège, Robert Torote, who, after initial hesitation, accepted the proposal of Juliana and her companions and first introduced the Solemnity of *Corpus Christi* in his diocese. Later other Bishops, following his example, instituted this Feast in the territories entrusted to their pastoral care.

However, to increase their faith, the Lord often asks Saints to sustain trials. This also happened to Juliana, who had to bear the harsh opposition of certain members of the clergy and even of the superior on whom her monastery depended. Of her own free will, therefore, Juliana left the Convent of Mont-Cornillon with several companions. For ten years—from 1248 to 1258—she stayed as a guest at various monasteries of Cistercian sisters. She edified all with her humility; she had no words of criticism or reproach for her adversaries and continued zealously to spread Eucharistic worship. She died at Fosses-La-Ville, Belgium, in 1258. In the cell where she lay the Blessed Sacrament was exposed, and, according to her biographer's account, Juliana died contemplating, with a last effusion of love, Jesus in the Eucharist, whom she had always loved, honored, and adored.

Jacques Pantaléon of Troyes was also won over to the good cause of the Feast of *Corpus Christi* during his ministry as Archdeacon in Liège. It was he who, having become Pope with the name of Urban IV in 1264, instituted the Solemnity of *Corpus Christi* on the Thursday after Pentecost as a feast of precept for the universal Church. In the Bull of its institution, entitled *Transiturus de hoc mundo* (11 August 1264), Pope Urban even referred discreetly to Juliana's mystical experiences, corroborating their authenticity. He wrote: "Although the Eucharist is celebrated solemnly every day, we deem it fitting that at least once a year it be celebrated with greater honor and a solemn commemoration. Indeed, we grasp the other things we commemorate with our spirit and our mind, but this does not mean that we obtain their real presence. On the contrary, in this sacramental commemoration of Christ, even though in a different form, Jesus Christ is present with us in his own substance. While he was about to ascend into Heaven he said 'And lo, I am with you always, to the close of the age' (Matthew 28:20)."

The Pontiff made a point of setting an example by celebrating the solemnity of *Corpus Christi* in Orvieto, the town where he was then residing. Indeed, he ordered that the famous *Corporal* with the traces of the Eucharistic miracle which had occurred in Bolsena the previous year, 1263, be kept in the Orvieto Cathedral—where it still is today. While a priest was consecrating the bread and the wine, he was overcome by strong doubts about the Real Presence of the Body and Blood of Christ in the sacrament of the Eucharist. A few drops of blood began miraculously to ooze from the consecrated Host, thereby confirming what our faith professes. Urban IV asked one of the greatest theologians of history, Saint Thomas Aquinas—who at that time was accompanying the Pope and was in Orvieto—to compose the texts of the Liturgical Office for this great Feast. They are masterpieces, still in use in the Church today, in which theology and poetry are fused. These texts pluck at the heart-strings in an expression of praise and gratitude to the Most Holy Sacrament, while the mind, penetrating the mystery with wonder, recognizes in the Eucharist the Living and Real Presence of Jesus, of his Sacrifice of love that reconciles us with the Father and gives us salvation.

Although after the death of Urban IV the celebration of the Feast of *Corpus Christi* was limited to certain regions of France, Germany, Hungary, and Northern Italy, it was another Pontiff, John XXII, who in 1317 re-established it for the universal Church. Since then the Feast has experienced a wonderful development and is still deeply appreciated by the Christian people. I would like to affirm with joy that today there is a "Eucharistic springtime" in the Church: How many people pause in silence before the Tabernacle to engage in a loving conversation with Jesus! It is comforting to know that many groups of young people have rediscovered the beauty of praying in adoration before the Most Blessed Sacrament. I am thinking, for example, of our Eucharistic adoration in Hyde Park, London. I pray that this Eucharistic "springtime" may spread increasingly in every parish and in particular in Belgium, Saint Juliana's homeland. Venerable John Paul II said in his Encyclical *Ecclesia de Eucharistia*: "In many places, adoration of the Blessed Sacrament is also an important daily practice and becomes an inexhaustible source of holiness. The devout participation of the faithful in the Eucharistic procession on the Solemnity of the Body and Blood of Christ is a grace from the Lord which yearly brings joy to those who take part in it. Other positive signs of Eucharistic faith and love might also be mentioned" (no. 10).

In remembering Saint Juliana of Cornillon, let us also renew our faith in the Real Presence of Christ in the Eucharist. As we are taught by the *Compendium of the Catechism of the Catholic Church*, "Jesus Christ is present in the Eucharist in a unique and incomparable way. He is present in a true, real and substantial way, with his Body and his Blood, with his Soul and his Divinity. In the Eucharist, therefore, there is present in a sacramental way, that is, under the Eucharistic species of bread and wine, Christ whole and entire, God and Man" (no. 282).

Dear friends, fidelity to the encounter with the Christ in the Eucharist in Holy Mass on Sunday is essential for the journey of faith, but let us also seek to pay frequent visits to the Lord present in the Tabernacle! In gazing in adoration at the consecrated Host, we discover the gift of God's love, we discover Jesus' Passion and Cross and likewise his Resurrection. It is precisely through our gazing in adoration that the Lord draws us toward him into his mystery in order to transform us as he transforms the bread and the wine. The Saints never failed to find strength, consolation, and joy in the Eucharistic encounter. Let us repeat before the Lord present in the Most Blessed Sacrament the words of the Eucharistic hymn "*Adoro te devote*": [Devoutly I adore Thee]: Make me believe ever more in you, "Draw me deeply into faith, / Into Your hope, into Your love."

23

Saint Catherine of Siena

WEDNESDAY, 24 NOVEMBER 2010
Paul VI Hall

Dear Brothers and Sisters,

Today I would like to talk to you about a woman who played an eminent role in the history of the Church: Saint Catherine of Siena. The century in which she lived—the fourteenth—was a troubled period in the life of the Church and throughout the social context of Italy and Europe. Yet, even in the most difficult times, the Lord does not cease to bless his People, bringing forth Saints who give a jolt to minds and hearts, provoking conversion and renewal. Catherine is one of these and still today speaks to us and impels us to walk courageously toward holiness to be ever more fully disciples of the Lord.

Born in Siena in 1347, into a very large family, she died in Rome in 1380. When Catherine was sixteen years old, motivated by a vision of Saint Dominic, she entered the Third Order of the Dominicans, the female branch known as the *Mantellate*. While living at home, she confirmed her vow of virginity made privately when she was still an adolescent and dedicated herself to prayer, penance, and works of charity, especially for the benefit of the sick. When the fame of her holiness spread, it led to an intense activity of spiritual guidance for people from every walk of life: nobles and politicians, artists and ordinary people, consecrated men and women and religious, including Pope Gregory XI, who was living at Avignon in that period and whom she energetically and effectively urged to return to Rome.

She traveled widely to press for the internal reform of the Church and to foster peace among the States. It was also for this reason that Venerable Pope John Paul II chose to declare her Co-Patroness of Europe: may the Old Continent never forget the Christian roots that are at the origin of its progress and continue to draw from the Gospel the fundamental values that assure justice and harmony.

Like many of the Saints, Catherine knew great suffering. Some even thought that they should not trust her, to the point that in 1374, six years before her death, the General Chapter of the Dominicans summoned her to Florence to interrogate her. They appointed Raymund of Capua, a learned and humble friar and a future Master General of the Order, as her spiritual guide. Having become her confessor and also her "spiritual son", he wrote a first complete biography of the Saint. She was canonized in 1461.

The teaching of Catherine, who learned to read with difficulty and learned to write in adulthood, is contained in the *Dialogue of Divine Providence*, or *Libro della Divina Dottrina*, a masterpiece of spiritual literature, in her *Epistolario*, and in the collection of her *Prayers*. Her teaching is endowed with such excellence that in 1970 the Servant of God Paul VI declared her a Doctor of the Church, a title that was added to those of Co-Patroness of the City of Rome—at the wish of Blessed Pius IX—and of Patroness of Italy—in accordance with the decision of Venerable Pius XII.

In a vision that was ever present in Catherine's heart and mind, Our Lady presented her to Jesus, who gave her a splendid ring, saying to her: "I, your Creator and Savior, espouse you in the faith, which you will keep ever pure until you celebrate your eternal nuptials with me in Heaven" (Blessed Raimondo da Capua, *S. Caterina da Siena, Legenda maior*, no. 115, Siena, 1998). This ring was visible to her alone. In this extraordinary episode, we see the vital center of Catherine's religious sense and of all authentic spirituality: Christocentrism. For her, Christ was like the spouse with whom a relationship of intimacy, communion, and faithfulness exists; he was the best beloved whom she loved above any other good.

This profound union with the Lord is illustrated by another episode in the life of this outstanding mystic: the exchange of hearts. According to Raymund of Capua, who passed on the confidences Catherine received, the Lord Jesus appeared to her "holding in his holy hands a human heart, bright red and shining". He opened her side and put the heart within her, saying: "Dearest daughter, as I took your heart away from you the other day, now, you see, I am giving you mine, so that you can go on living with it forever" (*ibid.*). Catherine truly lived Saint Paul's words, "It is no longer I who live, but Christ who lives in me" (Gal 2:20).

Like the Sienese Saint, every believer feels the need to be conformed to the sentiments of the heart of Christ in order to love God and his neighbor as Christ himself loves. And we can all let our hearts be transformed and learn to love like Christ in a familiarity with him that is nourished by prayer, by meditation on the word of God, and by the sacraments, above all by receiving Holy Communion frequently and with devotion. Catherine also belongs to the throng of Saints devoted to the Eucharist with which I concluded my Apostolic Exhortation *Sacramentum Caritatis* (cf. no. 94).

Dear brothers and sisters, the Eucharist is an extraordinary gift of love that God continually renews to nourish our journey of faith, to strengthen our hope, and to inflame our charity, to make us more and more like him. A true and authentic spiritual family was built up around such a strong and genuine personality; people fascinated by the moral authority of this young woman with a most exalted lifestyle were at times also impressed by the mystical phenomena they witnessed, such as her frequent ecstasies. Many put themselves at Catherine's service and above all considered it a privilege to receive spiritual guidance from her. They called her "mother" because, as her spiritual children, they drew spiritual nourishment from her.

Today, too, the Church receives great benefit from the exercise of spiritual motherhood by so many women, lay and consecrated, who nourish souls with thoughts of God, who strengthen the people's faith and direct Christian life toward ever loftier peaks. "Son, I say to you and call you", Catherine wrote to one of her spiritual sons, Giovanni Sabbatini, a Carthusian, "inasmuch as I give birth to you in continuous prayers and desire in the presence of God, just as a mother gives birth to a son" (*Epistolario*, *Lettera*, no. 141: *To Fr. Giovanni de' Sabbatini*). She would usually address the Dominican Father Bartolomeo de Dominici with these words: "Most beloved and very dear brother and son in Christ sweet Jesus".

Another trait of Catherine's spirituality is linked to the gift of tears. They express an exquisite, profound sensitivity, a capacity for being moved and for tenderness. Many Saints have had the gift of tears, renewing the emotion of Jesus himself, who did not hold back or hide his tears at the tomb of his friend Lazarus and at the grief of Mary and Martha or at the sight of Jerusalem during his last days on this earth. According to Catherine, the tears of Saints are mingled with the blood of Christ, of which she spoke in vibrant tones and with symbolic images that were very effective: "Remember Christ crucified, God and man. . . . Make your aim the Crucified Christ, hide in the wounds of the Crucified Christ, and drown in the blood of the Crucified Christ" (*Epistolario, Lettera*, no. 16: *Ad uno il cui nome si tace* [to one who remains anonymous]).

Here we can understand why, despite her awareness of the human shortcomings of priests, Catherine always felt very great reverence for them: through the sacraments and the word, they dispense the saving power of Christ's Blood. The Sienese Saint always invited the sacred ministers, including the Pope, whom she called "sweet Christ on earth", to be faithful to their responsibilities, motivated always and only by her profound and constant love of the Church. She said before she died: "In leaving my body, truly I have consumed and given my life in the Church and for the Holy Church, which is for me a most unique grace" (*Raimondo da Capua, S. Caterina da Siena, Legenda maior*, no. 363).

Hence we learn from Saint Catherine the most sublime science: to know and love Jesus Christ and his Church. In the *Dialogue of Divine Providence*, she describes Christ, with an unusual image, as a bridge flung between Heaven and earth. This bridge consists of three great stairways constituted by the feet, the side, and the mouth of Jesus. Rising by these stairways, the soul passes through the three stages of every path to sanctification: detachment from sin, the practice of the virtues and of love, and sweet and loving union with God.

Dear brothers and sisters, let us learn from Saint Catherine to love Christ and the Church with courage, intensely and sincerely. Therefore let us make our own Saint

Catherine's words that we read in the *Dialogue of Divine Providence* at the end of the chapter that speaks of Christ as a bridge: "Out of mercy you have washed us in his Blood, out of mercy you have wished to converse with creatures. O crazed with love! It did not suffice for you to take flesh, but you also wished to die! . . . O mercy! My heart drowns in thinking of you: for no matter where I turn my thoughts, I find only mercy" (chap. 30, pp. 79–80).

24

Julian of Norwich

WEDNESDAY, 1 DECEMBER 2010
Paul VI Hall

Dear Brothers and Sisters,

I still remember with great joy the Apostolic Journey I made in the United Kingdom last September. England is a land that has given birth to a great many distinguished figures who enhanced Church history with their testimony and their teaching. One of them, venerated both in the Catholic Church and in the Anglican Communion, is the mystic Julian of Norwich, of whom I wish to speak this morning.

The—very scant—information on her life in our possession comes mainly from her *Revelations of Divine Love in Sixteen Showings*, the book in which this kindly and devout woman set down the content of her visions. It is known that she lived from 1342 until about 1430, turbulent years both for the Church, torn by the schism that followed the Pope's return to Rome from Avignon, and for the life of the people, who were suffering the consequences of a long, drawn-out war between the Kingdoms of England and of France. God, however, even in periods of tribulation, does not cease to inspire figures such as Julian of Norwich to recall people to peace, love, and joy.

As Julian herself recounts, in May 1373, most likely on the thirteenth of that month, she was suddenly stricken with a very serious illness that in three days seemed to be carrying her to the grave. After the priest, who hastened to her bedside, had shown her the Crucified One, not only did Julian rapidly recover her health, but she received the sixteen revelations that she subsequently wrote down and commented on in her book, *Revelations of Divine Love*. And it was the Lord himself, fifteen years after these extraordinary events, who revealed to her the meaning of those visions. "'Would you learn to see clearly your Lord's meaning in this thing? Learn it well: Love was his meaning. Who showed it to you? Love.... Why did he show it to you? For Love'.... Thus I was taught that Love was our Lord's meaning" (Julian of Norwich, *Revelations of Divine Love*, chap. 86).

Inspired by divine love, Julian made a radical decision. Like an ancient anchoress, she decided to live in a cell located near the church called after Saint Julian, in the city of Norwich—in her time an important urban center not far from London. She may have taken the name of Julian precisely from that Saint to whom was dedicated the church in whose vicinity she lived for so many years, until her death. This decision to live as a "recluse", the term in her day, might surprise or even perplex us. But she was not the only one to make such a choice. In those centuries a considerable number of women opted for this form of life, adopting rules specially drawn up for them, such as the rule compiled by Saint Aelred of Rievaulx. The anchoresses, or "recluses", in their cells, devoted themselves to prayer, meditation, and study. In this way they developed a highly refined human and religious sensitivity which earned them the veneration of the people. Men and women of every age and condition in need of advice and comfort would devoutly seek them. It was not, therefore, an individualistic choice; precisely with this closeness to the Lord, Julian developed the ability to be a counselor to a great many people and to help those who were going through difficulties in this life.

We also know that Julian, too, received frequent visitors, as is attested by the autobiography of another fervent Christian of her time, Margery Kempe, who went to Norwich in 1413 to receive advice on her spiritual life. This is why, in her lifetime, Julian was called "Dame Julian", as is engraved on the funeral monument that contains her remains. She had become a mother to many.

Men and women who withdraw to live in God's company acquire by making this decision a great sense of compassion for the suffering and weakness of others. As friends of God, they have at their disposal a wisdom that the world—from which they have distanced themselves—does not possess, and they amiably share it with those who knock at their door. I therefore recall with admiration and gratitude the women and men's cloistered monasteries. Today more than ever they are oases of peace and hope, a precious treasure for the whole Church, especially since they recall the primacy of God and the importance, for the journey of faith, of constant and intense prayer.

It was precisely in the solitude infused with God that Julian of Norwich wrote her *Revelations of Divine Love*. Two versions have come down to us, one that is shorter, probably the older, and one that is longer. This book contains a message of optimism based on the certainty of being loved by God and of being protected by his Providence. In this book we read the following wonderful words: "And I saw full surely that ere God made us he loved us; which love was never lacking nor ever shall be. And in this love he has made all his works; and in this love he has made all things profitable to us; and in this love our life is everlasting . . . in which love we have our beginning. And all this shall we see in God, without end" (*Revelations of Divine Love*, chap. 86). The theme of divine love recurs frequently in the visions of Julian of Norwich, who, with a certain daring, did not hesitate to compare it also to motherly love. This is one of the most characteristic messages of her mystical theology. The tenderness, concern, and gentleness of God's kindness to us are so great that they remind us, pilgrims on earth, of a mother's love for her children. In fact, the biblical prophets also sometimes used this language that calls to mind the tenderness, intensity, and totality of God's love, which is manifested in creation and in the whole history of salvation, crowned by the Incarnation of the Son. God, however, always excels all human love, as the Prophet Isaiah says: "Can a woman forget her sucking child, that she should have no compassion on the son of her womb? Even these may forget, yet I will never forget you" (Is 49:15). Julian of Norwich understood the central message for spiritual life: God is love, and it is only if one opens oneself to this love, totally and with total trust, and lets it become one's sole guide in life that all things are transfigured, that true peace and true joy are found, and that one is able to radiate it.

I would like to emphasize another point. The *Catechism of the Catholic Church* cites the words of Julian of Norwich when it explains the viewpoint of the Catholic faith on an argument that never ceases to be a provocation to all believers (cf. nos. 304–13, 314). If God is supremely good and wise, why do evil and the suffering of innocents exist? And the Saints themselves asked this very question. Illumined by faith, they give an answer that opens our hearts to trust and hope: in the mysterious designs of Providence,

God can draw a greater good even from evil, as Julian of Norwich wrote: "Here I was taught by the grace of God that I should steadfastly keep me in the faith . . . and that . . . I should take my stand on and earnestly believe in . . . that 'all manner [of] thing shall be well'" (*The Revelations of Divine Love*, chap. 32).

Yes, dear brothers and sisters, God's promises are ever greater than our expectations. If we present to God, to his immense love, the purest and deepest desires of our heart, we shall never be disappointed. "And all will be well", "all manner of things shall be well": this is the final message that Julian of Norwich transmits to us and that I am also proposing to you today.

25

Saint Catherine of Bologna

WEDNESDAY, 29 DECEMBER 2010
Paul VI Hall

Dear Brothers and Sisters,

In a recent Catechesis I spoke of Saint Catherine of Siena. Today I would like to present to you another less well known Saint who has the same name: Saint Catherine of Bologna, a very erudite yet very humble woman. She was dedicated to prayer but was always ready to serve; generous in sacrifice but full of joy in welcoming Christ with the Cross.

Catherine was born in Bologna on 8 September 1413, the eldest child of Benvenuta Mammolini and John de' Vigri, a rich and cultured patrician of Ferrara, a doctor in law and a public lector in Padua, where he carried out diplomatic missions for Nicholas III d'Este, Marquis of Ferrara. Not much information about Catherine's infancy and child hood is available, and not all of it is reliable. As a child she lived in her grandparents' house in Bologna, where she was brought up by relatives, especially by her mother, who was a woman of deep faith. With her, Catherine moved to Ferrara when she was about ten years old and entered the court of Nicholas III d'Este as lady-in-waiting to Margaret, Nicholas' illegitimate daughter. The Marquis was transforming Ferrara into a fine city, summoning artists and scholars from various countries. He encouraged culture and, although his private life was not exemplary, took great care of the spiritual good, moral conduct, and education of his subjects.

In Ferrara Catherine was unaware of the negative aspects that are often part and parcel of court life. She enjoyed Margaret's friendship and became her confidante. She developed her culture by studying music, painting, and dancing; she learned to write poetry and literary compositions and to play the viola; she became expert in the art of miniature-painting and copying; she perfected her knowledge of Latin. In her future monastic life she was to put to good use the cultural and artistic heritage she had acquired in these years. She learned with ease, enthusiasm, and tenacity. She showed great prudence, as well as an unusual modesty, grace, and kindness in her behavior. However, one absolutely clear trait distinguished her: her spirit, constantly focused on the things of Heaven. In 1427, when she was only fourteen years old and subsequent to certain family events, Catherine decided to leave the court to join a group of young noblewomen who lived a community life, dedicating themselves to God. Her mother trustingly consented in spite of having other plans for her daughter.

We know nothing of Catherine's spiritual path prior to this decision. Speaking in the third person, she states that she entered God's service, "illumined by divine grace ... with an upright conscience and great fervor", attentive to holy prayer by night and by day, striving to acquire all the virtues she saw in others, "not out of envy, but the better to please God, in whom she had placed all her love" (*Le sette armi necessarie alla battaglia spirituali* [The seven spiritual weapons], VII, 8, Bologna, 1998, p. 12). She made considerable spiritual progress in this new phase of her life, but her trials, her inner suffering, and especially the temptations of the devil were great and terrible. She passed through a profound spiritual crisis and came to the brink of despair (cf. *ibid.*, VII, 2, pp. 12–29). She lived in the night of the spirit and was also deeply shaken by the temptation of disbelief in the Eucharist. After so much suffering, the Lord comforted her: he gave her, in a vision, a clear awareness of the Real Presence in the Eucharist, an awareness so dazzling that Catherine was unable to express it in words (cf. *ibid.*, VIII, 2, pp. 42–46). In this same period a sorrowful trial afflicted the community: tension arose between those who wished to follow the Augustinian spirituality and those who had more of an inclination for Franciscan spirituality.

Between 1429 and 1430, Lucia Mascheroni, in charge of the group, decided to found an Augustinian monastery. Catherine, on the other hand, chose with others to bind herself to the Rule of Saint Clare of Assisi. It was a gift of Providence, because the community dwelled in the vicinity of the Church of the Holy Spirit, annexed to the convent of the Friars Minor who had adhered to the movement of the Observance. Thus Catherine and her companions could take part regularly in liturgical celebrations and receive adequate spiritual assistance. They also had the joy of listening to the preaching of Saint Bernardine of Siena (cf. *ibid.*, VII, 62, p. 26). Catherine recounts that in 1429—the third year after her conversion—she went to make her confession to one of the Friars Minor whom she esteemed; she made a good confession and prayed the Lord intensely to grant her forgiveness for all her sins and the suffering connected with them. In a vision God revealed to her that he had forgiven her everything. It was a very strong experience of divine mercy that left an indelible mark upon her, giving her a fresh impetus to respond generously to God's immense love (cf. *ibid.*, IX, 2, pp. 46–48).

In 1431 she had a vision of the Last Judgment. The terrifying spectacle of the damned impelled her to redouble her prayers and penance for the salvation of sinners. The devil continued to assail her, and she entrusted herself ever more totally to the Lord and to the Virgin Mary (cf. *ibid.*, X, 3, pp. 53–54). In her writings, Catherine has left us a few essential notes concerning this mysterious battle from which, with God's grace, she emerged victorious. She did so in order to instruct her sisters and those who intend to set out on the path of perfection: she wanted to put them on their guard against the temptations of the devil, who often conceals himself behind deceptive guises, later to sow doubts about faith, vocational uncertainty, and sensuality.

In her autobiographical and didactic treatise *The Seven Spiritual Weapons*, Catherine offers in this regard teaching of deep wisdom and profound discernment. She speaks in the third person in reporting the extraordinary graces which the Lord gives to her and in the first person in confessing her sins. Her writing reveals the purity of her faith in God, her profound humility, the simplicity of her heart, her missionary zeal, her passion for the salvation of souls. She identifies seven weapons in the fight against evil, against the devil: 1. always to be careful and diligently strive to do good; 2. to believe that alone we will never be able to do anything truly good; 3. to trust in God and, for love of him, never to fear in the battle against evil, either in the world or within ourselves; 4. to meditate often on the events and words of the life of Jesus, and especially on his Passion and his death; 5. to remember that we must die; 6. to focus our minds firmly on memory of the goods of Heaven; 7. to be familiar with Sacred Scripture, always cherishing it in our hearts so that it may give direction to all our thoughts and all our actions. A splendid program of spiritual life, today too, for each one of us!

In the convent Catherine, in spite of being accustomed to the court in Ferrara, served in the offices of laundress, dressmaker, and breadmaker and even looked after the animals. She did everything, even the lowliest tasks, with love and ready obedience, offering her sisters a luminous witness. Indeed, she saw disobedience as that spiritual pride which destroys every other virtue. Out of obedience she accepted the office of novice mistress, although she considered herself unfit for this office, and God continued to inspire her with his presence and his gifts: in fact she proved to be a wise and appreciated mistress.

Later the service of the parlor was entrusted to her. She found it trying to have to interrupt her prayers frequently in order to respond to those who came to the monastery grill, but this time, too, the Lord did not fail to visit her and to be close to her. With her the monastery became an increasingly prayerful place of self-giving, of silence, of endeavor, and of joy. Upon the death of the abbess, the superiors thought immediately of her, but Catherine urged them to turn to the Poor Clares of Mantua, who were better instructed in the Constitutions and in religious observance. Nevertheless, a few years later, in 1456, she was asked at her monastery to open a new foundation in Bologna. Catherine would have preferred to end her days in Ferrara, but the Lord appeared to her and exhorted her to do God's will by going to Bologna as abbess. She prepared herself for the new commitment with fasting, scourging, and penance. She went to Bologna with eighteen sisters. As superior she set the example in prayer and in service; she lived in deep humility and poverty. At the end of her three-year term as abbess, she was glad to be replaced, but after a year she was obliged to resume her office because the newly elected abbess became blind. Although she was suffering and was afflicted with serious ailments that tormented her, she carried out her service with generosity and dedication.

For another year she urged her sisters to an evangelical life, to patience and constancy in trial, to fraternal love, to union with the divine Bridegroom, Jesus, so as to prepare her dowry for the eternal nuptials. It was a dowry that Catherine saw as knowing how to share the sufferings of Christ, serenely facing hardship, apprehension, contempt, and misunderstanding (cf. *Le sette armi spirituali* X, 20, pp. 57–58). At the beginning of 1463, her health deteriorated. For the last time she gathered the sisters in Chapter in order to announce her death to them and to recommend the observance of the Rule. Toward the end of February, she was harrowed by terrible suffering that was never to leave her, yet despite her pain, it was she who comforted her sisters, assuring them that she would also help them from Heaven. After receiving the last sacraments, she gave her confessor the text she had written: *The Seven Spiritual Weapons*, and entered her agony; her face grew beautiful and translucent; she still looked lovingly at those who surrounded her and died gently, repeating three times the name of Jesus. It was 9 March 1463 (cf. I. Bembo, *Specchio di illuminazione, Vita di S. Caterina a Bologna*, Florence, 2001, chap. 3). Catherine was to be canonized by Pope Clement XI on 22 May 1712. Her incorrupt body is preserved in the city of Bologna, in the chapel of the monastery of Corpus Domini.

Dear friends, with her words and with her life, Saint Catherine of Bologna is a pressing invitation to let ourselves always be guided by God, to do his will daily, even if it often does not correspond with our plans, to trust in his Providence, which never leaves us on our own. In this perspective, Saint Catherine speaks to us; from the distance of so many centuries she is still very modern and speaks to our lives. She, like us, suffered temptations; she suffered the temptations of disbelief, of sensuality, of a difficult spiritual struggle. She felt forsaken by God; she found herself in the darkness of faith. Yet in all these situations, she was always holding the Lord's hand; she did not leave him; she did not abandon him. And walking hand in hand with the Lord, she walked on the right path and found the way of light. So it is that she also tells us: take heart, even in the night of faith, even amidst our many doubts, do not let go of the Lord's hand, walk hand in hand with him, believe in God's goodness. This is how to follow the right path! And I would like to stress another aspect: her great humility. She was a person who did not want to be someone or something; she did not care for appearances; she did not want to govern. She wanted to serve, to do God's will, to be at the service of others. And for this very reason Catherine was credible in her authority, because she was able to see that for her authority meant, precisely, serving others. Let us ask God, through the intercession of our Saint, for the gift to achieve courageously and generously the project he has for us, so that he alone may be the firm rock on which our lives are built.

26

Saint Catherine of Genoa

WEDNESDAY, 12 JANUARY 2011

Paul VI Hall

Dear Brothers and Sisters,

After Catherine of Siena and Catherine of Bologna, today I would like to speak to you about another Saint: Catherine of Genoa, known above all for her vision of Purgatory. The text that describes her life and thought was published in this Ligurian city in 1551. It is in three sections: her *Vita* [Life], properly speaking, the *Dimostratione et dechiaratione del purgatorio*—better known as the *Treatise on Purgatory*—and her *Dialogo tra l'anima e il corpo* (cf. *Libro de la Vita mirabile et dottrina santa, de la beata Caterinetta da Genoa: Nel quale si contiene una utile et catholica dimostratione et dechiaratione del purgatorio*, Genoa, 1551). The final version was written by Catherine's confessor, Father Cattaneo Marabotto.

Catherine was born in Genoa in 1447. She was the youngest of five. Her father, Giacomo Fieschi, died when she was very young. Her mother, Francesca di Negro, provided such an effective Christian education that the elder of her two daughters became a religious. When Catherine was sixteen, she was given in marriage to Giuliano Adorno, a man who after various trading and military experiences in the Middle East had returned to Genoa in order to marry.

Married life was far from easy for Catherine, partly because of the character of her husband, who was given to gambling. Catherine herself was at first induced to lead a worldly sort of life, in which, however, she failed to find serenity. After ten years, her heart was heavy with a deep sense of emptiness and bitterness.

A unique experience on 20 March 1473 sparked her conversion. She had gone to the Church of San Benedetto in the monastery of Nostra Signora delle Grazie [Our Lady of Grace] to make her confession and, kneeling before the priest, "received", as she herself wrote, "a wound in my heart from God's immense love". It came with such a clear vision of her own wretchedness and shortcomings and at the same time of God's goodness that she almost fainted. Her heart was moved by this knowledge of herself—knowledge of the empty life she was leading and of the goodness of God. This experience prompted the decision that gave direction to her whole life. She expressed it in the words: "no longer the world, no longer sin" (cf. *Vita Mirabile*, 3rv). Catherine did not stay to make her confession. On arriving home, she entered the most remote room and spent a long time weeping. At that moment she received an inner instruction on prayer and became aware of God's immense love for her, a sinner. It was a spiritual experience she had no words to describe (cf. *Vita Mirabile*, 4r). It was on this occasion that the suffering Jesus appeared to her, bent beneath the Cross, as he is often portrayed in the Saint's iconography. A few days later she returned to the priest to make a good confession at last. It was here that began the "life of purification" which for many years caused her to feel constant sorrow for the sins she had committed and which spurred her to impose forms of penance and sacrifice upon herself, in order to show her love to God.

On this journey Catherine became ever closer to the Lord until she attained what is called "unitive life", namely, a relationship of profound union with God. In her *Vita* it is written that her soul was guided and instructed from within solely by the sweet love of God, which gave her all she needed. Catherine surrendered herself so totally into the hands of the Lord that she lived, for about twenty-five years, as she wrote, "without the assistance of any creature, taught and governed by God alone" (*Vita*, 117r–118r), nourished above all by constant prayer and by Holy Communion, which she received every day, an unusual practice in her time. Only many years later did the Lord give her a priest who cared for her soul.

Catherine was always reluctant to confide and reveal her experience of mystical communion with God, especially because of the deep humility she felt before the Lord's graces. The prospect of glorifying him and of being able to contribute to the spiritual journey of others alone spurred her to recount what had taken place within her, from the moment of her conversion, which is her original and fundamental experience. The place of her ascent to mystical peaks was Pammatone Hospital, the largest hospital complex in Genoa, of which she was director and animator. Hence Catherine lived a totally active existence despite the depth of her inner life. In Pammatone a group of followers, disciples, and collaborators formed around her, fascinated by her life of faith and her charity. Indeed, her husband, Giuliano Adorno, was so won over that he gave up his dissipated life, became a Third Order Franciscan, and moved into the hospital to help his wife. Catherine's dedication to caring for the sick continued until the end of her earthly life on 15 September 1510. From her conversion until her death, there were no extraordinary events; rather, two elements characterize her entire life: on the one hand, her mystical experience, that is, the profound union with God, which she felt as spousal union, and, on the other, assistance to the sick, the organization of the hospital, and service to her neighbor, especially the neediest and the most forsaken. These two poles, God and neighbor, totally filled her life, virtually all of which she spent within the hospital walls.

Dear friends, we must never forget that the more we love God and the more constantly we pray, the better we will succeed in truly loving those who surround us, who are close to us, so that we can see in every person the Face of the Lord, whose love knows no bounds and makes no distinctions. The mystic does not create distance from others or an abstract life but, rather, approaches other people so that they may begin to see and act with God's eyes and heart.

Catherine's thought on Purgatory, for which she is particularly well known, is summed up in the last two parts of the book mentioned above: the *Treatise on Purgatory* and the *Dialogues between the Body and the Soul.* It is important to note that Catherine, in her mystical experience, never received specific revelations on Purgatory or on the souls being purified there. Yet, in the writings inspired by our Saint, Purgatory is a central element, and the description of it has characteristics that were original in her time. The first original passage concerns the "place" of the purification of souls. In her day it was depicted mainly using images linked to space: a certain space was conceived of in which Purgatory was supposed to be located. Catherine, however, did not see Purgatory as a scene in the bowels of the earth: for her it is not an exterior but rather an interior fire. This is Purgatory: an inner fire. The Saint speaks of the soul's journey of purification on the way to full communion with God, starting from her own experience of profound sorrow for the sins committed, in comparison with God's infinite love (cf. *Vita Mirabile*, 171v). We heard of the moment of conversion when Catherine suddenly became aware of God's goodness, of the infinite distance of her own life from this goodness, and of a burning fire within her. And this is the fire that purifies, the interior fire of Purgatory. Here, too, is an original feature in comparison with the thought of her time. In fact, she does not start with the afterlife in order to recount the torments of Purgatory—as was the custom in her time and perhaps still is today—and then to point out the way to purification or conversion. Rather, our Saint begins with the inner experience of her own life on the way to eternity. "The soul", Catherine says, "presents itself to God still bound to the desires and suffering that derive from sin, and this makes it impossible for it to enjoy the beatific vision of God." Catherine asserts that God is so pure and holy that a soul stained by sin cannot be in the presence of the divine majesty (cf. *Vita Mirabile*, 177r). We too feel how distant we are, how full we are of so many things that we cannot see God. The soul is aware of the immense love and perfect justice of God and consequently suffers for having failed to respond in a correct and perfect way to this love; and love for God itself becomes a flame; love itself cleanses it from the residue of sin.

In Catherine we can make out the presence of theological and mystical sources on which it was normal to draw in her time. In particular, we find an image typical of Dionysius the Areopagite: the thread of gold that links the human heart to God himself. When God purifies man, he binds him with the finest golden thread, that is, his love, and draws him toward himself with such strong affection that man is, as it were, "overcome and won over and completely beside himself". Thus man's heart is pervaded by God's love, which becomes the one guide, the one driving force of his life (cf. *Vita Mirabile*, 246rv). This situation of being uplifted toward God and of surrender to his will, expressed in the image of the thread, is used by Catherine to express the action of divine light on the souls in Purgatory, a light that purifies and raises them to the splendor of the shining radiance of God (cf. *Vita Mirabile*, 179r).

Dear friends, in their experience of union with God, Saints attain such a profound knowledge of the divine mysteries in which love and knowledge interpenetrate that they are of help to theologians themselves in their commitment to study, to *intelligentia fidei*, to an *intelligentia* of the mysteries of faith, to attain a really deeper knowledge of the mysteries of faith, for example, of what Purgatory is. With her life, Saint Catherine teaches us that the more we love God and enter into intimacy with him in prayer, the more he makes himself known to us, setting our hearts on fire with his love. In writing about Purgatory, the Saint reminds us of a fundamental truth of faith that becomes for us an invitation to pray for the deceased so that they may attain the beatific vision of God in the Communion of Saints (cf. *Catechism of the Catholic Church*, no. 1032). Moreover, the humble, faithful, and generous service in Pammatone Hospital that the Saint rendered throughout her life is a shining example of charity for all and an encouragement, especially for women, who, with their precious work enriched by their sensitivity and attention to the poorest and neediest, make a fundamental contribution to society and to the Church.

27

Saint Joan of Arc

WEDNESDAY, 26 JANUARY 2011
Paul VI Hall

Dear Brothers and Sisters,

Today I would like to talk to you about Joan of Arc, a young Saint who lived at the end of the Middle Ages who died at the age of nineteen, in 1431. This French Saint, mentioned several times in the *Catechism of the Catholic Church*, is particularly close to Saint Catherine of Siena, Patroness of Italy and of Europe, of whom I spoke in a recent Catechesis. They were in fact two young women of the people, lay women consecrated in virginity, two committed mystics, not in the cloister, but in the midst of the most dramatic reality of the Church and the world of their time. They are perhaps the most representative of those "strong women" who, at the end of the Middle Ages, fearlessly bore the great light of the Gospel in the complex events of history. We could liken them to the holy women who stayed on Calvary, close to the Crucified Jesus and to Mary, his Mother, while the Apostles had fled and Peter himself had denied him three times. The Church in that period was going through the profound crisis of the great schism of the West, which lasted almost forty years. In 1380, when Catherine of Siena died, there was not only a Pope but also an antipope; when Joan was born, in 1412, there was a Pope as well as two antipopes. In addition to this internal laceration in the Church were the continuous fratricidal wars among the Christian peoples of Europe, the most dramatic of which was the protracted Hundred Years' War between France and England.

Joan of Arc did not know how to read or write, but the depths of her soul can be known thanks to two sources of exceptional historical value: the two *Trials* that concern her. The first, the *Trial of Condemnation* (*PCon*), contains the transcription of the long and numerous interrogations to which Joan was subjected in the last months of her life (February–May 1431) and reports the Saint's own words. The second, the *Trial of Nullity of the Condemnation* or of "rehabilitation" (*PNul*), contains the depositions of about 120 eyewitnesses of all the periods of her life (cf. *Procès de Condamnation de Jeanne d'Arc*, 3 vols., and *Procès en Nullité de la Condamnation de Jeanne d'Arc*, 5 vols., ed. Klincksieck, Paris, 1960–1989).

Joan was born at Domrémy, a little village on the border between France and Lorraine. Her parents were well-off peasants, known to all as good Christians. From them she received a sound religious upbringing, considerably influenced by the spirituality of the *Name of Jesus*, taught by Saint Bernardine of Siena and spread in Europe by the Franciscans. The *Name of Mary* was always associated with the Name of Jesus, and thus, against the background of popular piety, Joan's spirituality was profoundly Christocentric and Marian. From childhood, she showed great love and compassion for the poorest, the sick, and all the suffering, in the dramatic context of the war.

We know from Joan's own words that her religious life developed as a mystical experience from the time when she was thirteen (*PCon* I, pp. 47–48). Through the "voice" of Saint Michael the Archangel, Joan felt called by the Lord to intensify her Christian life and also to commit herself personally to the liberation of her people. Her immediate response, her "yes", was her vow of virginity, with a new commitment to sacramental life and to prayer: daily participation in Mass, frequent confession and Communion, and long periods of silent prayer before the Crucified One or the image of Our Lady. The young French peasant girl's compassion and dedication in the face of her people's suffering were intensified by her mystical relationship with God. One of the most original aspects of this young woman's holiness was precisely this link between mystical experience and political mission. The years of her hidden life and her interior development were followed by the brief but intense two years of her public life: a year of *action* and a year of *passion*. At the beginning of 1429, Joan began her work of liberation. The many witnesses show us this young woman who was only seventeen years old as a very strong and determined person, able to convince people who felt insecure and discouraged. Overcoming all obstacles, she met the Dauphin of France, the future King Charles VII, who subjected her to an examination in Poitiers by some theologians of the university. Their opinion was positive: they saw in her nothing evil, only a good Christian.

On 22 March 1429, Joan dictated an important letter to the King of England and to his men at arms who were besieging the city of Orléans (*ibid.*, pp. 221–22). Hers was a true proposal of peace in justice between the two Christian peoples in light of the Names of Jesus and Mary, but it was rejected, and Joan had to gird herself to fight for the city's liberation, which took place on 8 May. The other culminating moment of her political action was the coronation of King Charles VII in Rheims on 17 July 1429. For a whole year, Joan lived with the soldiers, carrying out among them a true mission of evangelization. Many of them testified to her goodness, her courage, and her extraordinary purity. She was called by all and by herself "la pucelle" ("the Maid"), that is, virgin.

Joan's *passion* began on 23 May 1430, when she fell into enemy hands and was taken prisoner. On 23 December she was led to the city of Rouen. There the long and dramatic *Trial of Condemnation* took place, which began in February 1431 and ended on 30 May with her being burned at the stake. It was a great and solemn Trial, at which two ecclesiastical judges presided, Bishop Pierre Cauchon and the Inquisitor Jean le Maistre, but in fact it was conducted entirely by a large group of theologians from the renowned University of Paris, who took part in the Trial as assessors. They were French clerics who, on the side politically opposed to Joan's, had *a priori* a negative opinion of both her and her mission. This Trial is a distressing page in the history of holiness and also an illuminating page on the mystery of the Church, which, according to the words of the Second Vatican Council, is "at once holy and always in need of purification" (*Lumen Gentium*, no. 8). The Trial was the dramatic encounter between this Saint and her judges, who were clerics. Joan was accused and convicted by them, even condemned as a heretic and sent to the terrible death of being burned at the stake. Unlike the holy theologians who had illuminated the University of Paris, such as Saint Bonaventure, Saint Thomas Aquinas, and Blessed Duns Scotus, of whom I have spoken in several Catecheses, these judges were theologians who lacked charity and the humility to see God's action in this young woman. The words of Jesus, who said that God's mysteries are revealed to those who have a child's heart, while they remain hidden to the learned and the wise who have no humility (cf. Lk 10:21), spring to mind. Thus, Joan's judges were radically incapable of understanding her or of perceiving the beauty of her soul. They did not know that they were condemning a Saint.

Joan's appeal to the Pope, on 24 May, was rejected by the tribunal. On the morning of 30 May, in prison, she received Holy Communion for the last time and was immediately led to her torture in the Old Market Square. She asked one of the priests to hold up a processional Cross in front of the stake. Thus she died, her gaze fixed upon the Crucified Jesus and crying out several times the Name of Jesus (*PNul* I, p. 457; cf. *Catechism of the Catholic Church*, no. 435). About twenty-five years later, the *Trial of Nullity*, which opened under the authority of Pope Calixtus III, ended with a solemn sentence that declared the condemnation null and void (7 July 1456; *PNul* II, pp. 604–10). This long Trial, which collected the evidence of witnesses and the opinions of many theologians, all favorable to Joan, sheds light on her innocence and on her perfect fidelity to the Church. Joan of Arc was subsequently canonized by Benedict XV in 1920.

Dear brothers and sisters, the *Name of Jesus*, invoked by our Saint until the very last moments of her earthly life, was like the continuous breathing of her soul, like the beating of her heart, the center of her whole life. *The Mystery of the Charity of Joan of Arc* which so fascinated the poet Charles Péguy was this total love for Jesus and for her neighbor in Jesus and for Jesus. This Saint had understood that Love embraces the whole of the reality of God and of the human being, of Heaven and of earth, of the Church and of the world. Jesus always had pride of place in her life, in accordance with her beautiful affirmation: "We must serve God first" (*PCon* I, p. 288; cf. *Catechism of the Catholic Church*, no. 223). Loving him means always doing his will. She declared with total surrender and trust: "I entrust myself to God my Creator, I love him with my whole heart" (*PCon* I, p. 337). With the vow of virginity, Joan consecrated her whole being exclusively to the one Love of Jesus: "It was the promise that she made to Our Lord to preserve the virginity of her body and her mind well" (*PCon* I, pp. 149–50). Virginity of soul is the *state of grace*, a supreme value, for her more precious than life. It is a gift of God which is to be received and preserved with humility and trust. One of the best-known texts of the first *Trial* concerns precisely this: "Asked if she knew that she was in God's grace, she replied: 'If I am not, may it please God to put me in it; if I am, may it please God to keep me there'" (*ibid.*, p. 62; cf. *Catechism of the Catholic Church*, no. 2005).

Our Saint lived prayer in the form of a continuous dialogue with the Lord, who also illuminated her dialogue with the judges and gave her peace and security. She asked him with trust: "Sweetest God, in honor of your holy Passion, I ask you, if you love me, to show me how I must answer these men of the Church" (*PCon* I, p. 252). Joan saw Jesus as the "King of Heaven and of the earth". She therefore had painted on her standard the image of "Our Lord holding the world" (*ibid.*, p. 172): the emblem of her political mission. The liberation of her people was a work of human justice which Joan carried out in charity, for love of Jesus. Her holiness is a beautiful example for lay people engaged in politics, especially in the most difficult situations. Faith is the light that guides every decision, as a century later another great Saint, the Englishman Thomas More, was to testify. In Jesus Joan contemplated the whole reality of the Church, the "Church triumphant" of Heaven, as well as the "Church militant" on earth. According to her words,

"About Jesus Christ and the Church, I simply know they're just one thing" (*ibid.*, p. 166). This affirmation, cited in the *Catechism of the Catholic Church* (no. 795), has a truly heroic character in the context of the *Trial of Condemnation*, before her judges, men of the Church who were persecuting and condemning her. In the Love of Jesus Joan found the strength to love the Church to the very end, even at the moment she was sentenced. I like to recall that Saint Joan of Arc had a profound influence on a young Saint of the modern age: Thérèse of the Child Jesus. In the context of a completely different life, spent in the cloister, the Carmelite of Lisieux felt very close to Joan, living in the heart of the Church and participating in Christ's suffering for the world's salvation. The Church has brought them together as Patronesses of France, after the Virgin Mary. Saint Thérèse expressed her desire to die, like Joan, with the Name of Jesus on her lips (*Manuscript B*, 3r), and she was motivated by the same great love for Jesus and her neighbor, lived in consecrated virginity.

Dear brothers and sisters, with her luminous witness Saint Joan of Arc invites us to a high standard of Christian living: to make prayer the guiding motive of our days; to have full trust in doing God's will, whatever it may be; to live charity without favoritism, without limits, and drawing, like her, from the Love of Jesus a profound love for the Church.

28

Saint Teresa of Avila

WEDNESDAY, 2 FEBRUARY 2011
Paul VI Audience Hall

Dear Brothers and Sisters,

In the course of the Catecheses that I have chosen to dedicate to the Fathers of the Church and to great theologians and women of the Middle Ages, I have also had the opportunity to reflect on certain saints proclaimed Doctors of the Church on account of the eminence of their teaching. Today I would like to begin a brief series of meetings to complete the presentation on the Doctors of the Church, and I am beginning with a Saint who is one of the peaks of Christian spirituality of all time—Saint Teresa of Avila [also known as Saint Teresa of Jesus].

Saint Teresa, whose name was Teresa de Cepeda y Ahumada, was born in Avila, Spain, in 1515. In her autobiography she mentions some details of her childhood: she was born into a large family with a "father and mother who were devout and feared God". She had three sisters and nine brothers. While she was still a child and not yet nine years old, she had the opportunity to read the lives of several Martyrs which inspired in her such a longing for martyrdom that she briefly ran away from home in order to die a Martyr's death and to go to Heaven (cf. *Vida* [*Life*] 1, 4);

"I want to see God", the little girl told her parents. A few years later, Teresa was to speak of her childhood reading and to state that she had discovered in it the way of truth which she sums up in two fundamental principles. On the one hand was the fact that "all things of this world will pass away", while on the other God alone is "for ever, ever, ever", a topic that recurs in her best-known poem: "Let nothing disturb you, Let nothing frighten you, All things are passing away: God never changes. Patience obtains all things. Whoever has God lacks nothing; God alone suffices." She was about twelve years old when her mother died and she implored the Virgin Most Holy to be her mother (cf. *Vida* 1, 7).

If in her adolescence the reading of profane books had led to the distractions of a worldly life, her experience as a pupil of the Augustinian nuns of Santa María de las Gracias de Avila and her reading of spiritual books, especially the classics of Franciscan spirituality, introduced her to recollection and prayer. When she was twenty, she entered the Carmelite Monastery of the Incarnation, also in Avila. In her religious life, she took the name "Teresa of Jesus". Three years later, she fell seriously ill, so ill that she remained in a coma for four days, looking as if she were dead (cf. *Vida* 5, 9). In the fight against her own illnesses, too, the Saint saw the combat against weaknesses and the resistance to God's call: "I wished to live," she wrote, "but I saw clearly that I was not living but, rather, wrestling with the shadow of death; there was no one to give me life, and I was not able to take it. He who could have given it to me had good reasons for not coming to my aid, seeing that he had brought me back to himself so many times, and I as often had left him" (*Vida* 7, 8). In 1543 she lost the closeness of her relatives; her father died, and all her siblings, one after another, emigrated to America. In Lent 1554, when she was thirty-nine years old, Teresa reached the climax of her struggle against her own weaknesses. The fortuitous discovery of the statue of "a Christ most grievously wounded" left a deep mark on her life (cf. *Vida* 9). The Saint, who in that period felt deeply in tune with the Saint Augustine of the *Confessions*, thus describes the decisive day of her mystical experience: "and . . . a feeling of the presence of God would come over me unexpectedly, so that I could in no wise doubt either that he was within me or that I was wholly absorbed in him" (*Vida* 10, 1).

Parallel to her inner development, the Saint began in practice to realize her ideal of the reform of the Carmelite Order: in 1562 she founded the first reformed Carmel in Avila, with the support of the city's Bishop, Don Alvaro de Mendoza, and shortly afterward also received the approval of John Baptist Rossi, the Order's Superior General. In the years that followed, she continued her foundations of new Carmelite convents, seventeen in all. Her meeting with Saint John of the Cross was fundamental. With him, in 1568, she set up the first convent of Discalced Carmelites in Duruelo, not far from Avila. In 1580, she obtained from Rome the authorization for her reformed Carmels as a separate, autonomous Province. This was the starting point for the Discalced Carmelite Order. Indeed, Teresa's earthly life ended while she was in the middle of her founding activities. She died on the night of 15 October 1582 in Alba de Tormes, after setting up the Carmelite Convent in Burgos, while on her way back to Avila. Her last humble words were: "After all I die as a daughter of the Church", and "O my Lord and my Spouse, the hour that I have longed for has come. It is time to meet one another." Teresa spent her entire life for the whole Church although she spent it in Spain. She was beatified by Pope Paul V in 1614 and canonized by Gregory XV in 1622. The Servant of God Paul VI proclaimed her a "Doctor of the Church" in 1970.

Teresa of Jesus had no academic education but always set great store by the teachings of theologians, men of letters, and spiritual teachers. As a writer, she always adhered to what she had lived through personally or had seen in the experience of others (cf. *Prologue* to *The Way of Perfection*), in other words, basing herself on her own first-hand knowledge. Teresa had the opportunity to build up relations of spiritual friendship with many saints and with Saint John of the Cross in particular. At the same time she nourished herself by reading the Fathers of the Church, Saint Jerome, Saint Gregory the Great, and Saint Augustine. Among her most important works we should mention first of all her autobiography, *El libro de la vida* [The Book of (Her) Life], which she called *Libro de las misericordias del Señor* [Book of the Lord's Mercies]. Written in the Carmelite Convent at Avila in 1565, she describes the biographical and spiritual journey, as she herself says, to submit her soul to the discernment of the "Master of things spiritual", Saint John of Avila. Her purpose was to highlight the presence and action of the merciful God in her life. For this reason the work often cites her dialogue in prayer with the Lord. It makes fascinating reading because not only does the Saint recount that she is reliving the profound experience of her relationship with God, but she also demonstrates it. In 1566, Teresa wrote *El Camino de Perfección* [The Way of Perfection]. She called it *Advertencias y consejos que da Teresa de Jesús a sus hermanas* [recommendations and advice that Teresa of Jesus offers to her sisters]. It was composed for the twelve novices of the

Carmel of Saint Joseph in Avila. Teresa proposes to them an intense program of contemplative life at the service of the Church, at the root of which are the evangelical virtues and prayer. Among the most precious passages is her commentary on the *Our Father*, as a model for prayer. Saint Teresa's most famous mystical work is *El Castillo interior* [The Interior Castle]. She wrote it in 1577, when she was in her prime. It is a reinterpretation of her own spiritual journey and, at the same time, a codification of the possible development of Christian life toward its fullness, holiness, under the action of the Holy Spirit. Teresa refers to the structure of a castle with seven rooms as an image of human interiority. She simultaneously introduces the symbol of the silk worm reborn as a butterfly, in order to express the passage from the natural to the supernatural. The Saint draws inspiration from Sacred Scripture, particularly the Song of Songs, for the final symbol of the "Bride and Bridegroom" which enables her to describe, in the seventh room, the four crowning aspects of Christian life: the Trinitarian, the Christological, the anthropological, and the ecclesial. Saint Teresa devoted the *Libro de la fundaciones* [Book of the Foundations], which she wrote between 1573 and 1582, to her activity as Foundress of the reformed Carmels. In this book she speaks of the life of the nascent religious group. This account, like her autobiography, was written above all in order to give prominence to God's action in the work of founding new monasteries.

It is far from easy to sum up in a few words Teresa's profound and articulate spirituality. I would like to mention a few essential points. In the first place, Saint Teresa proposes the evangelical virtues as the basis of all Christian and human life and, in particular, detachment from possessions, that is, evangelical poverty, and this concerns all of us; love for one another as an essential element of community and social life; humility as love for the truth; determination as a fruit of Christian daring; theological hope, which she describes as the thirst for living water. Then we should not forget the human virtues: affability, truthfulness, modesty, courtesy, cheerfulness, culture. Secondly, Saint Teresa proposes a profound harmony with the great biblical figures and eager listening to the word of God. She feels above all closely in tune with the Bride in the Song of Songs and with the Apostle Paul, as well as with Christ in the Passion and with Jesus in the Eucharist.

The Saint then stresses how essential prayer is. Praying, she says, "means being on terms of friendship with God, frequently conversing in secret with him who, we know, loves us" (*Vida* 8, 5). Saint Teresa's idea coincides with Thomas Aquinas' definition of theological charity as "amicitia quaedam hominis ad Deum", a type of human friendship with God, who offered humanity his friendship first; it is from God that the initiative comes (cf. *Summa Theologiae* II-II, 23, 1). Prayer is life and develops gradually, in pace with the growth of Christian life: it begins with vocal prayer, passes through interiorization by means of meditation and recollection, until it attains the union of love with Christ and with the Holy Trinity. Obviously, in the development of prayer, climbing to the highest steps does not mean abandoning the previous type of prayer. Rather, it is a gradual deepening of the relationship with God that envelops the whole of life. Rather than a pedagogy, Teresa's is a true "mystagogy" of prayer: she teaches those who read her works how to pray by praying with them. Indeed, she often interrupts her account or exposition with a prayerful outburst.

Another subject dear to the Saint is the centrality of Christ's humanity. For Teresa, in fact, Christian life is the personal relationship with Jesus that culminates in union with him through grace, love, and imitation. Hence the importance she attaches to meditation on the Passion and on the Eucharist as the presence of Christ in the Church for the life of every believer and as the heart of the liturgy. Saint Teresa lives out unconditional love for the Church: she shows a lively *"sensus Ecclesiae"* in the face of the episodes of division and conflict in the Church of her time. She reformed the Carmelite Order with the intention of serving and defending the "Holy Roman Catholic Church" and was willing to give her life for the Church (cf. *Vida* 33, 5).

A final essential aspect of Teresian doctrine which I would like to emphasize is perfection, as the aspiration of the whole of Christian life and as its ultimate goal. The Saint has a very clear idea of the "fullness" of Christ, relived by the Christian. At the end of the route through *The Interior Castle*, in the last "room", Teresa describes this fullness, achieved in the indwelling of the Trinity, in union with Christ through the mystery of his humanity.

Dear brothers and sisters, Saint Teresa of Jesus is a true teacher of Christian life for the faithful of every time. In our society, which all too often lacks spiritual values, Saint Teresa teaches us to be unflagging witnesses of God, of his presence and of his action. She teaches us truly to feel this thirst for God that exists in the depths of our hearts, this desire to see God, to seek God, to be in conversation with him, and to be his friends. This is the friendship we all need, which we must seek anew, day after day. May the example of this Saint, profoundly contemplative and effectively active, spur us, too, every day to dedicate the right time to prayer, to this openness to God, to this journey, in order to seek God, to see him, to discover his friendship, and so to find true life; indeed, many of us should truly say: "I am not alive, I am not truly alive, because I do not live the essence of my life." Therefore time devoted to prayer is not time wasted, it is time in which the path of life unfolds, the path unfolds to learning from God an ardent love for him, for his Church, and practical charity for our brothers and sisters.

29

Saint Peter Canisius

WEDNESDAY, 9 FEBRUARY 2011
Paul VI Audience Hall

Dear Brothers and Sisters,

Today I want to talk to you about Saint Peter Kanis, Canisius in the Latin form of his surname, a very important figure of the Catholic sixteenth century. He was born on 8 May 1521 in Wijmegen, Holland. His father was Burgomaster of the town. While he was a student at the University of Cologne, he regularly visited the Carthusian monks of Saint Barbara, a driving force of Catholic life, and other devout men who cultivated the spirituality of the so-called *devotio moderna* [modern devotion]. He entered the Society of Jesus on 8 May 1543 in Mainz (Rhineland—Palatinate), after taking a course of spiritual exercises under the guidance of Blessed Pierre Favre, Petrus [Peter] Faber, one of Saint Ignatius of Loyola's first companions. He was ordained a priest in Cologne. Already the following year, in June 1546, he attended the Council of Trent, as the theologian of Cardinal Otto Truchseß von Waldburg, Bishop of Augsberg, where he worked with two confreres, Diego Laínez and Alfonso Salmerón.

In 1548, Saint Ignatius had him complete his spiritual formation in Rome and then sent him to the College of Messina to carry out humble domestic duties. He earned a doctorate in theology at Bologna on 4 October 1549, and Saint Ignatius assigned him to carry out the apostolate in Germany. On 2 September of that same year he visited Pope Paul III at Castel Gandolfo and then went to Saint Peter's Basilica to pray. Here he implored the great Holy Apostles Peter and Paul for help to make the Apostolic Blessing permanently effective for the future of his important new mission. He noted several words of this prayer in his spiritual journal. He said: "There I felt that a great consolation and the presence of grace had been granted to me through these intercessors [Peter and Paul]. They confirmed my mission in Germany and seemed to transmit to me, as an apostle of Germany, the support of their benevolence. You know, Lord, in how many ways and how often on that same day you entrusted Germany to me, about which I was later to continue to be concerned and for which I would have liked to live and die."

We must bear in mind that we are dealing with the time of the Lutheran Reformation, at the moment when the Catholic faith in the German-speaking countries seemed to be dying out in the face of the fascination of the Reformation. The task of Canisius—charged with revitalizing or renewing the Catholic faith in the Germanic countries—was almost impossible. It was possible only by virtue of prayer. It was possible only from the center, namely, a profound personal friendship with Jesus Christ, a friendship with Christ in his Body, the Church, which must be nourished by the Eucharist, his Real Presence.

In obedience to the mission received from Ignatius and from Pope Paul III, Canisius left for Germany. He went first to the Duchy of Bavaria, which for several years was the place where he exercised his ministry. As dean, rector, and vice chancellor of the University of Ingolstadt, he supervised the academic life of the Institute and the religious and moral reform of the people. In Vienna, where for a brief time he was diocesan administrator, he carried out his pastoral ministry in hospitals and prisons, both in the city and in the countryside, and prepared the publication of his *Catechism*. In 1556, he founded the College of Prague and, until 1569, was the first superior of the Jesuit Province of Upper Germany.

In this office he established a dense network of communities of his Order in the Germanic countries, especially colleges, which were starting points for the Catholic Reformation, for the renewal of the Catholic faith. At that time he also took part in the Colloquy of Worms with Protestant divines, including Philipp Melanchthon (1557); he served as Papal Nuncio in Poland (1558); he took part in the two Diets of Augsberg (1559 and 1565); he accompanied Cardinal Stanislaw Hozjusz, Legate of Pope Pius IV, to Emperor Ferdinand (1560); and he took part in the last session of the Council of Trent, where he spoke on the issue of Communion under both Species and on the Index of Prohibited Books (1562).

In 1580, he withdrew to Fribourg, Switzerland, where he devoted himself entirely to preaching and writing. He died there on 21 December 1597. Blessed Pius IX beatified him in 1864, and in 1897 Pope Leo XIII proclaimed him the "Second Apostle of Germany". Pope Pius XI canonized him and proclaimed him a Doctor of the Church in 1925.

Saint Peter Canisius spent a large part of his life in touch with the most important people of his time and exercised a special influence with his writings. He edited the complete works of Cyril of Alexandria and of Saint Leo the Great, the Letters of Saint Jerome, and the Orations of Saint Nicholas of Flüe. He published devotional books in various languages, biographies of several Swiss saints, and numerous homiletic texts. However, his most widely disseminated writings were the three *Catechisms* he compiled between 1555 and 1558. The first *Catechism* was addressed to students who could grasp the elementary notions of theology; the second, to young people of the populace for an initial religious instruction; the third, to youth with a scholastic formation of middle and high school levels. He explained Catholic doctrine with questions and answers, concisely, in biblical terms, with great clarity and with no polemical overtones. There were at least two hundred editions of this *Catechism* in his lifetime alone! And hundreds of editions succeeded one another until the twentieth century. So it was that still in my father's generation people in Germany were calling the *Catechism* simply "*the Canisius*". He really was the *Catechist* of Germany; he formed people's faith for centuries.

This was a characteristic of Saint Peter Canisius: his ability to combine harmoniously fidelity to dogmatic principles with the respect that is due to every person. Saint Canisius distinguished between a conscious, blameworthy apostasy from faith and a blameless loss of faith through circumstances. Moreover, he declared to Rome that the majority of Germans who switched to Protestantism were blameless. In a historical period of strong confessional differences, Canisius avoided—and this is something quite extraordinary—the harshness and rhetoric of anger—something rare, as I said, in the discussions between Christians in those times—and aimed only at presenting the spiritual roots and at reviving the faith in the Church. His vast and penetrating knowledge of Sacred Scripture and of the Fathers of the Church served this cause: the same knowledge that supported his personal relationship with God and the austere spirituality that he derived from the *Devotio Moderna* and Rhenish mysticism.

Characteristic of Saint Canisius' spirituality was his profound personal friendship with Jesus. For example, on 4 September 1549 he wrote in his journal, speaking with the Lord: "In the end, as if you were opening to me the heart of the Most Sacred Body, which it seemed to me I saw before me, you commanded me to drink from that source, inviting me, as it were, to draw the waters of my salvation from your founts, O my Savior." Then he saw that the Savior was giving him a garment with three pieces that were called peace, love, and perseverance. And with this garment, made up of peace, love, and perseverance, Canisius carried out his work of renewing Catholicism. His friendship with Jesus—which was the core of his personality—nourished by love of the Bible, by love of the Blessed Sacrament, and by love of the Fathers, this friendship was clearly united with the awareness of being a perpetuator of the Apostles' mission in the Church. And this reminds us that every genuine evangelizer is always an instrument united with Jesus and with his Church and is fruitful for this very reason.

Friendship with Jesus had been inculcated in Saint Peter Canisius in the spiritual environment of the Charterhouse of Cologne, in which he had been in close contact with two Carthusian mystics: Johannes Lansperger, whose name has been Latinized as "Lanspergius", and Nikolaus van Esche, Latinized as "Eschius". He subsequently deepened the experience of this friendship, *familiaritas stupenda nimis*, through contemplation of the mysteries of Jesus' life, which form a large part of Saint Ignatius' Spiritual Exercises. This is the foundation of his intense devotion to the heart of the Lord, which culminated in his consecration to the apostolic ministry in the Vatican Basilica.

The Christocentric spirituality of Saint Peter Canisius is rooted in a profound conviction: no soul anxious for perfection fails to practice prayer daily, mental prayer, an ordinary means that enables the disciple of Jesus to live in intimacy with the divine Teacher. For this reason, in his writings for the spiritual education of the people, our Saint insists on the importance of the liturgy with his comments on the Gospels, on Feasts, on the Rite of Holy Mass, and on the sacraments; yet, at the same time, he is careful to show the faithful the need for and beauty of personal daily prayer, which should accompany and permeate participation in the public worship of the Church.

This exhortation and method have kept their value intact, especially after being authoritatively proposed anew by the Second Vatican Council in the Constitution *Sacrosanctum Concilium*: Christian life does not develop unless it is nourished by participation in the liturgy—particularly at Sunday Mass—and by personal daily prayer, by personal contact with God. Among the thousands of activities and multiple distractions that surround us, we must find moments for recollection before the Lord every day, in order to listen to him and speak with him.

At the same time, the example that Saint Peter Canisius has bequeathed to us, not only in his works but especially with his life, is ever timely and of lasting value. He teaches clearly that the apostolic ministry is effective and produces fruits of salvation in hearts only if the preacher is a personal witness of Jesus and an instrument at his disposal, bound to him closely by faith in his Gospel and in his Church, by a morally consistent life, and by prayer as ceaseless as love. And this is true for every Christian who wishes to live his adherence to Christ with commitment and fidelity.

30

Saint John of the Cross

WEDNESDAY, 16 FEBRUARY 2011
Paul VI Audience Hall

Dear Brothers and Sisters,

Two weeks ago I presented the figure of the great Spanish mystic Teresa of Jesus. Today I would like talk about another important saint of that country, a spiritual friend of Saint Teresa, the reformer, with her, of the Carmelite religious family: Saint John of the Cross. He was proclaimed a Doctor of the Church by Pope Pius XI in 1926 and is traditionally known as *Doctor mysticus*, "Mystical Doctor".

John of the Cross was born in 1542 in the small village of Fontiveros, near Avila in Old Castille, to Gonzalo de Yepes and Catalina Alvarez. The family was very poor because his father, Gonzalo, from a noble family of Toledo, had been thrown out of his home and disowned for marrying Catalina, a humble silk weaver. Having lost his father at a tender age, when John was nine he moved with his mother and his brother Francisco to Medina del Campo, not far from Valladolid, a commercial and cultural center. Here he attended the *Colegio de los Doctrinos*, carrying out in addition several humble tasks for the sisters of the Church-Convent of the Maddalena. Later, given his human qualities and his academic results, he was admitted first as a male nurse to the Hospital of the Conception, then to the recently founded Jesuit College at Medina del Campo. He entered the College at the age of eighteen and studied the humanities, rhetoric, and classical languages for three years. At the end of his formation, he had a clear perception of his vocation: the religious life, and, among the many orders present in Medina, he felt called to Carmel.

In the summer of 1563 he began his novitiate with the Carmelites in the town, taking the religious name of Juan de Santo Matía. The following year he went to the prestigious University of Salamanca, where he studied the humanities and philosophy for three years. He was ordained a priest in 1567 and returned to Medina del Campo to celebrate his first Mass surrounded by his family's love. It was precisely here that John and Teresa of Jesus first met. The meeting was crucial for them both. Teresa explained to him her plan for reforming Carmel, including the male branch of the Order, and suggested to John that he support it "for the greater glory of God". The young priest was so fascinated by Teresa's ideas that he became a great champion of her project. For several months they worked together, sharing ideals and proposals aiming to inaugurate the first house of Discalced Carmelites as soon as possible. It was opened on 28 December 1568 at Duruelo in a remote part of the Province of Avila. This first reformed male community consisted of John and three companions. In renewing their religious profession in accordance with the primitive Rule, each of the four took a new name: it was from this time that John called himself "of the Cross", as he came to be known subsequently throughout the world. At the end of 1572, at Saint Teresa's request, he became confessor and vicar of the Monastery of the Incarnation in Avila, where Teresa of Jesus was prioress. These were years of close collaboration and spiritual friendship which enriched both. The most important Teresian works and John's first writings date back to this period.

Promoting adherence to the Carmelite reform was far from easy and cost John acute suffering. The most traumatic episode occurred in 1577, when he was seized and imprisoned in the Carmelite Convent of the Ancient Observance in Toledo, following an unjust accusation. The Saint, imprisoned for months, was subjected to physical and moral deprivations and constrictions. Here, together with other poems, he composed the well-known *Spiritual Canticle*. Finally, in the night between 16 and 17 August 1578, he made a daring escape and sought shelter at the Monastery of Discalced Carmelite Nuns in the town. Saint Teresa and her reformed companions celebrated his liberation with great joy, and, after spending a brief period recovering, John was assigned to Andalusia, where he spent ten years in various convents, especially in Granada. He was charged with ever more important offices in his Order, until he became vicar provincial and completed the draft of his spiritual treatises. He then returned to his native land as a member of the General Government of the Teresian religious family, which already enjoyed full juridical autonomy. He lived in the Carmel of Segovia, serving in the office of community superior. In 1591, he was relieved of all responsibility and assigned to the new religious Province of Mexico. While he was preparing for the long voyage with ten companions, he retired to a secluded convent near Jaén, where he fell seriously ill. John faced great suffering with exemplary serenity and patience. He died in the night between 13 and 14 December 1591, while his confreres were reciting Matins. He took his leave of them saying: "Today I am going to sing the Office in Heaven."

His mortal remains were translated to Segovia. He was beatified by Clement X in 1675 and canonized by Benedict XIII in 1726.

John is considered one of the most important lyric poets of Spanish literature. His major works are four: *The Ascent of Mount Carmel*, *The Dark Night*, *The Spiritual Canticle*, and *The Living Flame of Love*.

In *The Spiritual Canticle*, Saint John presents the process of the soul's purification, that is, the gradual, joyful possession of God, until the soul succeeds in feeling that it loves God with the same love with which it is loved by him. *The Living Flame of Love* continues in this perspective, describing in greater detail the state of the transforming union with God. The example that John uses is always that of fire: just as the stronger the fire burns and consumes wood, the brighter it grows until it blazes into a flame, so the Holy Spirit, who purifies and "cleanses" the soul during the dark night, with time illuminates and warms it as though it were a flame. The life of the soul is a continuous celebration of the Holy Spirit which gives us a glimpse of the glory of union with God in eternity.

The Ascent of Mount Carmel presents the spiritual itinerary from the viewpoint of the gradual purification of the soul, necessary in order to scale the peaks of Christian perfection, symbolized by the summit of Mount Carmel. This purification is proposed as a journey the human being undertakes, collaborating with divine action, to free the soul from every attachment or affection contrary to God's will. Purification, which, if it is to attain the union of love with God, must be total, begins by purifying the life of the senses and continues with the life obtained through the three theological virtues: faith, hope, and charity, which purify the intention, the memory, and the will.

The Dark Night describes the "passive" aspect, that is, God's intervention in this process of the soul's "purification". In fact, human endeavor on its own is unable to reach the profound roots of the person's bad inclinations and habits: all it can do is to check them but cannot entirely uproot them. This requires the special action of God, which radically purifies the spirit and prepares it for the union of love with him. Saint John describes this purification as "passive" precisely because, although it is accepted by the soul, it is brought about by the mysterious action of the Holy Spirit, who, like a burning flame, consumes every impurity. In this state, the soul is subjected to every kind of trial as if it were in a dark night.

This information on the Saint's most important works helps us to approach the salient points of his vast and profound mystical doctrine, whose purpose is to describe a sure way to attain holiness, the state of perfection to which God calls us all. According to John of the Cross, all that exists, created by God, is good. Through creatures we may arrive at the discovery of the One who has left within them a trace of himself. Faith, in any case, is the one source given to the human being to know God as he is in himself, as the triune God. All that God wished to communicate to man, he said in Jesus Christ, his Word made flesh. Jesus Christ is the only and definitive way to the Father (cf. Jn 14:6). Any created thing is nothing in comparison to God and is worth nothing outside him; consequently, to attain to the perfect love of God, every other love must be conformed in Christ to the divine love.

From this derives the insistence of Saint John of the Cross on the need for purification and inner self-emptying in order to be transformed into God, which is the one goal of perfection. This "purification" does not consist in the mere physical absence of things or of their use; on the contrary, what makes the soul pure and free is the elimination of every disorderly dependence on things. All things should be placed in God as the center and goal of life.

Of course, the long and difficult process of purification demands a personal effort, but the real protagonist is God: all that the human being can do is to "prepare" himself, to be open to divine action, and not to set up obstacles to it. By living the theological virtues, human beings raise themselves and give value to their commitment. The growth of faith, hope, and charity keeps pace with the work of purification and with the gradual union with God until they are transformed in him. When it reaches this goal, the soul is immersed in Trinitarian life itself, so that Saint John affirms that it has reached the point of loving God with the same love with which he loves it, because he loves it in the Holy Spirit. For this reason the Mystical Doctor maintains that there is no true union of love with God that does not culminate in Trinitarian union. In this supreme state, the holy soul knows everything in God and no longer has to pass through creatures in order to reach him. The soul now feels bathed in divine love and rejoices in it without reserve.

Dear brothers and sisters, in the end the question is: does this Saint with his lofty mysticism, with this demanding journey toward the peak of perfection, have anything to say to us, to the ordinary Christian who lives in the circumstances of our life today, or is he an example, a model for only a few elect souls who are truly able to undertake this journey of purification, of mystical ascesis? To find the answer, we must first of all bear in mind that the life of Saint John of the Cross did not "float on mystical clouds"; rather he had a very hard life, practical and concrete, both as a reformer of the Order, in which he came up against much opposition, and as Provincial Superior as well as in his confreres' prison, where he was exposed to unbelievable insults and physical abuse. His life was hard, yet it was precisely during the months he spent in prison that he wrote one of his most beautiful works. And so we can understand that the journey with Christ, traveling with Christ, "the Way", is not an additional burden in our life, it is not something that would make our burden even heavier, but something quite different. It is a light, a power that helps us to bear it.

If a person bears great love in himself, this love gives him wings, as it were, and he can face all life's troubles more easily because he carries in himself this great light; this is faith: being loved by God and letting oneself be loved by God in Jesus Christ. Letting oneself be loved in this way is the light that helps us to bear our daily burden. And holiness is not a very difficult action of ours but means exactly this "openness": opening the windows of our soul to let in God's light, without forgetting God, because it is precisely in opening oneself to his light that one finds strength, one finds the joy of the redeemed. Let us pray the Lord to help us discover this holiness, to let ourselves be loved by God, who is our common vocation and the true redemption.

31

Saint Robert Bellarmine

WEDNESDAY, 23 FEBRUARY 2011
Paul VI Audience Hall

Dear Brothers and Sisters,

Saint Robert Bellarmine, about whom I would like to speak to you today, carries us back in thought to the time of the painful division of Western Christianity, when a grave political and religious crisis brought about the separation of entire nations from the Apostolic See.

Born on 4 October 1542 in Montepulciano near Siena, he was the nephew, on his mother's side, of Pope Marcellus II. He had an excellent formation in the humanities before entering the Society of Jesus on 20 September 1560. His philosophy and theology studies, at the Roman College in Padua and at Louvain, focused on Saint Thomas and the Fathers of the Church. They were crucial to his theological orientation. He was ordained a priest on 25 March 1570 and for a few years was professor of theology at Louvain. Later, summoned to Rome to teach at the Roman College, he was entrusted with the chair of apologetics. In the decade in which he held it (1576–1586), he compiled a course of lessons which subsequently formed the *Controversiae* [Controversies], a work whose clarity, rich content, and mainly historical tone earned it instant renown. The Council of Trent had just ended, and, in the face of the Protestant Reformation, the Catholic Church was impelled to reinforce and confirm her identity. Bellarmine's action fitted into this context. From 1588 to 1594, he was first spiritual director of the Jesuit students at the Roman College—among whom he met and gave direction to Saint Aloysius Gonzaga—then religious superior. Pope Clement VIII appointed Father Bellarmine Papal Theologian, consultor to the Holy Office, and rector of the College of Confessors at Saint Peter's. His short catechism, *Dottrina cristiana* [Christian doctrine], dates back to the two-year period 1597–1598. It was one of his most popular works.

Pope Clement VIII created him a cardinal on 3 March 1599, and on 18 March 1602 he was appointed Archbishop of Capua. He received episcopal ordination on 21 April that same year. In the three years in which he was a diocesan bishop, he distinguished himself by his zeal as a preacher in his cathedral, by his weekly visits to parishes, by three Diocesan Synods, and by a Provincial Council which he founded. After taking part in the Conclaves that elected Pope Leo XI and Pope Paul V, he was called to Rome again, where he became a member of the Congregations of the Holy Office, of the Index, for Rites, for Bishops, and for the Propagation of the Faith. He also had diplomatic responsibilities in the Republic of Venice and in England to defend the rights of the Apostolic See. In his last years, he composed various books on spirituality in which he summarized the results of his annual spiritual exercises. Christian people today still draw great edification from reading them. He died in Rome on 17 September 1621. Pope Pius XI beatified him in 1923, canonized him in 1930, and proclaimed him a Doctor of the Church in 1931.

Saint Robert Bellarmine carried out an important role in the Church of the last decades of the sixteenth century and the first of decades of seventeenth. His *Controversiae* were a reference point, still valid, for Catholic ecclesiology on questions concerning revelation, the nature of the Church, the sacraments, and theological anthropology. In them the institutional aspect of the Church is emphasized because of the errors that were then circulating on these issues.

Nevertheless, Bellarmine also explained the invisible aspects of the Church as the Mystical Body and illustrated them with the analogy of body and soul in order to describe the relationship between the Church's inner riches and the external aspects that enable her to be perceived. In this monumental work that endeavors to organize the theological controversies of that time, he avoids any polemical and aggressive approach in speaking of the ideas of the Reformation. Instead, using the arguments of reason and the Tradition of the Church, he illustrates the Catholic doctrine clearly and effectively.

Yet his inheritance consists in the way in which he conceived of his work. Indeed, the burdensome offices of governance did not prevent him from striving daily for holiness, faithful to the demands of his own state as a religious, priest, and bishop. From this fidelity came his commitment to preaching assiduously.

Since, as a priest and bishop, he was first and foremost a pastor of souls, he felt it was his duty to preach diligently. He gave hundreds of *sermones*—homilies—in Flanders, Rome, Naples, and Capua during liturgical celebrations. Equally prolific were his *expositiones* and his *explanationes* to the parish priests, women religious, and students of the Roman College on Sacred Scripture and especially on Saint Paul's Letters. His preaching and his catechesis are always focused on what is essential, which he had learned from his Ignatian education, entirely directed to concentrating the soul's energies on the Lord Jesus intensely known, loved, and imitated.

In the writings of this man of governance, one is clearly aware, despite the reserve behind which he conceals his sentiments, of the primacy he gives to Christ's teaching. Saint Bellarmine thus offers a model of prayer, the soul of every activity: a prayer that listens to the word of God, that is satisfied in contemplating his grandeur, that does not withdraw into self but is pleased to abandon itself to God. A hallmark of Bellarmine's spirituality is his vivid personal perception of God's immense goodness. This is why our Saint truly felt he was a beloved son of God. It was a source of great joy to him to pause in recollection, with serenity and simplicity, in prayer and in contemplation of God. In his book *De ascensione mentis in Deum* [Elevation of the mind to God] composed in accordance with the plan of the *Itinerarium* [Journey of the mind into God] of Saint Bonaventure, he exclaims: "O soul, your example is God, infinite beauty, light without shadow, splendor that exceeds that of the moon and the sun. He raised his eyes to God, in whom is found the archetypes of all things and of whom, as from a source of infinite fertility, derives this almost infinite variety of things. For this reason you must conclude: whoever finds God finds everything, whoever loses God loses everything."

In this text an echo of the famous *contemplatio ad amorem obtineundum* [contemplation in order to obtain love] of the Spiritual Exercises of Saint Ignatius of Loyola can be heard. Bellarmine, who lived in the lavish and often unhealthy society of the end of late sixteenth and early seventeenth centuries, drew from this contemplation practical applications and applied them to the situation of the Church of his time with a lively pastoral inspiration. In his book *De arte bene moriendi* [The art of dying a good death], for example, he points out as a reliable norm for a good life and also for a good death that one regularly and seriously meditate on the fact that one must account to God for one's actions and one's way of life and seek not to accumulate riches on this earth but, rather, to live simply and charitably in such a way as to lay up treasure in Heaven. In his book *De gemitu columbae* [The lament of the dove], in which the dove represents the Church, is a forceful appeal to all the clergy and faithful to undertake a personal and concrete reform of their own life in accordance with the teachings of Scripture and of the saints, among whom he mentions in particular Saint Gregory Nazianzen, Saint John Crysostom, Saint Jerome, and Saint Augustine, as well as the great founders of religious orders, such as Saint Benedict, Saint Dominic, and Saint Francis. Bellarmine teaches with great clarity and with the example of his own life that there can be no true reform of the Church unless there is first our own personal reform and the conversion of our own heart.

Bellarmine found in the Spiritual Exercises of Saint Ignatius recommendations for communicating the profound beauty of the mysteries of faith, even to the simplest of people. He wrote:

> If you have wisdom, may you understand that you have been created for the glory of God and for your eternal salvation. This is your goal, this is the center of your soul, this the treasure of your heart. Therefore consider as truly good for you what leads you to your goal and truly evil what causes you to miss it. The wise person must not seek felicitous or adverse events, wealth or poverty, health or sickness, honors or offenses, life or death. They are good and desirable only if they contribute to the glory of God and to

your eternal happiness; they are evil and to be avoided if they hinder it. (*De ascensione mentis in Deum*, grad. 1.)

These are obviously not words that have gone out of fashion but words on which we should meditate at length today, to direct our journey on this earth. They remind us that the aim of our life is the Lord God who revealed himself in Jesus Christ, in whom he continues to call us and to promise us communion with him. They remind us of the importance of trusting in the Lord, of expending ourselves in a life faithful to the Gospel, of accepting and illuminating every circumstance and every action of our life with faith and with prayer, ever reaching for union with him.

32

Saint Francis de Sales

WEDNESDAY, 2 MARCH 2011
Paul VI Audience Hall

Dear Brothers and Sisters,

"God is God of the human heart" (*The Treatise on the Love of God* I, XV). These apparently simple words give us an impression of the spirituality of a great teacher of whom I would like to speak to you today: Saint Francis de Sales, a Bishop and Doctor of the Church. Born in 1567, in a French border region, he was the son of the Lord of Boisy, an ancient and noble family of Savoy. His life straddled two centuries, the sixteenth and seventeenth, and he summed up in himself the best of the teachings and cultural achievements of the century drawing to a close, reconciling the heritage of humanism striving for the Absolute that is proper to mystical currents. He received a very careful education; he undertook higher studies in Paris, where he dedicated himself to theology, and at the University of Padua, where he studied jurisprudence, complying with his father's wishes and graduating brilliantly with degrees in *utroque iure*, in canon law and in civil law. In his harmonious youth, reflection on the thought of Saint Augustine and of Saint Thomas Aquinas led to a deep crisis. This prompted him to question his own eternal salvation and the predestination of God concerning himself; he suffered as a true spiritual drama the principal theological issues of his time. He prayed intensely but was so fiercely tormented by doubt that for a few weeks he could barely eat or sleep. At the climax of his trial, he went to the Dominicans' church in Paris, opened his heart, and prayed in these words: "Whatever happens, Lord, you who hold all things in your hand and whose ways are justice and truth; whatever you have ordained for me ... you who are ever a just judge and a merciful Father, I will love you Lord.... I will love you here, O my God, and I will always hope in your mercy and will always repeat your praise.... O Lord Jesus, you will always be my hope and my salvation in the land of the living" (I *Proc. Canon.*, vol. I, art. 4). The twenty-year-old Francis found peace in the radical and liberating love of God: loving him without asking anything in return and trusting in divine love; no longer asking what will God do with me: I simply love him, independently of all that he gives me or does not give me. Thus I find peace, and the question of predestination—which was being discussed at that time—was resolved, because he no longer sought what he might receive from God; he simply loved God and abandoned himself to his goodness. And this was to be the secret of his life which would shine out in his main work: the *The Treatise on the Love of God*.

Overcoming his father's resistance, Francis followed the Lord's call and was ordained a priest on 18 December 1593. In 1602, he became Bishop of Geneva, in a period in which the city was the stronghold of Calvinism so that his episcopal see was transferred, "in exile", to Annecy. As the Pastor of a poor and tormented diocese in a mountainous area whose harshness was as well known as its beauty, he wrote: "I found [God] sweet and gentle among our loftiest rugged mountains, where many simple souls love him and worship him in all truth and sincerity; and mountain goats and chamois leap here and there between the fearful frozen peaks to proclaim his praise" (*Letter to Mother de Chantal*, October 1606, in *Oeuvres*, éd. Mackey, t. XIII, p. 223). Nevertheless, the influence of his life and his teaching on Europe in that period and in the following centuries is immense. He was an apostle, preacher, writer, man of action and of prayer, dedicated to implanting the ideals of the Council of Trent; he was involved in controversial issues and in dialogue with the Protestants, experiencing increasingly, over and above the necessary theological confrontation, the effectiveness of personal relationship and of charity; he was charged with diplomatic missions in Europe and with social duties of mediation and reconciliation. Yet above all, Saint Francis de Sales was a director: from his encounter with a young woman, Madame de Charmoisy, he was to draw the inspiration to write one of the most widely read books of the modern age, *The Introduction to a Devout Life*. A new religious family was to come into being from his profound spiritual communion with an exceptional figure, Saint Jane Frances de Chantal: the Order of the Visitation, as the Saint wished, was characterized by total consecration to God lived in simplicity and humility, in doing ordinary things extraordinarily well: "I want my Daughters", he wrote, "not to have any other ideal than that of glorifying [our Lord] with their humility" (*Letter to Bishop de Marquemond*, June 1615). He died in 1622, at the age of fifty-five, after a life marked by the hardness of the times and by his apostolic effort.

The life of Saint Francis de Sales was a relatively short life but was lived with great intensity. The figure of this Saint radiates an impression of rare fullness, demonstrated in the serenity of his intellectual research but also in the riches of his affection and the "sweetness" of his teachings, which had an important influence on the Christian conscience. He embodied the different meanings of the word "humanity" which this term can assume today, as it could in the past: culture and courtesy, freedom and tenderness, nobility and solidarity. His appearance reflected something of the majesty of the landscape in which he lived and preserved its simplicity and naturalness. Moreover, the words of the past and the images he used resonate unexpectedly in the ears of men and women today, as a native and familiar language.

To Philothea, the ideal person to whom he dedicated his *Introduction to a Devout Life* (1607), Francis de Sales addressed an invitation that might well have seemed revolutionary at the time. It is the invitation to belong completely to God, while living to the full her presence in the world and the tasks proper to her state. "My intention is to teach those who are living in towns, in the conjugal state, at court" (*Preface* to *The Introduction to a Devout Life*). The Document with which Pope Leo XIII, more than two centuries later, was to proclaim him a Doctor of the Church would insist on this expansion of the call to perfection, to holiness. It says: "[True piety] shone its light everywhere and gained entrance to the thrones of kings, the tents of generals, the courts of judges, custom houses, workshops, and even the huts of herdsmen" (cf. Brief, *Dives in Misericordia*, 16 November 1877). Thus came into being the appeal to lay people and the care for the consecration of temporal things and for the sanctification of daily life on which the Second Vatican Council and the spirituality of our time were to insist. The ideal of a reconciled humanity was expressed in the harmony between prayer and action in the world, between the search for perfection and the secular condition, with the help of God's grace, which permeates the human being and, without destroying him, purifies him, raising him to divine heights. To Theotimus, the spiritually mature Christian adult to whom a few years later he addressed his *Treatise on the Love of God*, Saint Francis de Sales offered a more complex lesson. At the beginning it presents a precise vision of the human being, an anthropology: human "reason", indeed "our soul in so far as it is reasonable", is seen there as harmonious architecture, a temple, divided into various courts around a center, which, together with the great mystics, he calls the "extremity and summit of our soul, this highest point of our spirit". This is the point where reason, having ascended all its steps, "closes its eyes" and knowledge becomes one with love (cf. Book I, chap. XII). The fact that love in its theological and divine dimension may be the *raison d'être* of all things, on an ascending ladder that does not seem to experience breaks or abysses, Saint Francis de Sales summed up in a famous sentence: "Man is the perfection of the universe; the spirit is the perfection of man; love, that of the spirit; and charity, that of love" (*ibid.*, book X, chap. 1).

In an intensely flourishing season of mysticism, *The Treatise on the Love of God* was a true and proper *summa* and at the same time a fascinating literary work. Saint Francis' description of the journey toward God starts from recognition of the "natural inclination" (*ibid.*, book I, chap. XVI), planted in man's heart—although he is a sinner—to love God above all things. According to the model of Sacred Scripture, Saint Francis de Sales speaks of the union between God and man, developing a whole series of images and interpersonal relationships. His God is Father and Lord, husband and friend, who has the characteristics of mother and of wet-nurse and is the sun of which even the night is a mysterious revelation. Such a God draws man to himself with bonds of love, namely, true freedom, for: "love has neither convicts nor slaves, but brings all things under its obedience with a force so delightful that, as nothing is so strong as love, nothing also is so sweet as its strength" (*ibid.*, book I, chap. VI). In our Saint's *Treatise*, we find a profound meditation on the human will and the description of its flowing, passing, and dying in order to live (cf. *ibid.*, book IX, chap. XIII) in complete surrender not only to God's will but also to what pleases him, to his "bon plaisir", his good pleasure (cf. *ibid.*, book IX, chap. I). As well as by raptures of contemplative ecstasy, union with God is crowned by that reappearance of charitable action which is attentive to all the needs of others and which he calls "the ecstasy of action and life" (*ibid.*, book VII, chap. VI).

In reading his book on the love of God and especially his many letters of spiritual direction and friendship, one clearly perceives that Saint Francis was well acquainted with the human heart. He wrote to Saint Jane de Chantal: ". . . this is the rule of our obedience, which I write for you in capital letters: do all through love, nothing through constraint; love obedience more than you fear disobedience. I leave you the spirit of freedom, not that which excludes obedience, which is the freedom of the world, but that liberty which excludes violence, anxiety, and scruples" (*Letter* of 14 October 1604). It is not for nothing that we rediscover traces precisely of this teacher at the origin of many contemporary paths of pedagogy and spirituality; without him neither Saint John Bosco nor the heroic "Little Way" of Saint Thérèse of Lisieux would have come into being.

Dear brothers and sisters, in an age such as ours that seeks freedom, even with violence and unrest, we must not miss the timeliness of this great teacher of spirituality and peace, who gave his followers the "spirit of freedom", the true spirit. Saint Francis de Sales is an exemplary witness of Christian humanism; with his familiar style, with words which at times have a poetic touch, he reminds us that human beings have planted in their innermost depths the longing for God and that in him alone can they find true joy and the most complete fulfillment.

33

Saint Lawrence of Brindisi

WEDNESDAY, 23 MARCH 2011
Saint Peter's Square

Dear Brothers and Sisters,

I still remember with joy the festive welcome I was given in Brindisi in 2008. It was in this city that in 1559 was born a distinguished Doctor of the Church, Saint Lawrence of Brindisi, the name that Julius Caesar Russo took upon entering the Capuchin Order. He had been attracted since childhood by the family of Saint Francis of Assisi. In fact, his father died when he was seven years old, and his mother entrusted him to the care of the Friars Minor Conventual in his hometown. A few years later, however, Lawrence and his mother moved to Venice, and it was precisely there that he became acquainted with the Capuchins, who in that period were generously dedicated to serving the whole Church in order to further the important spiritual reform promoted by the Council of Trent. With his religious profession in 1575, Lawrence became a Capuchin friar, and in 1582 he was ordained a priest. During his ecclesiastical studies for the priesthood, he already showed the eminent intellectual qualities with which he had been endowed. He learned with ease the ancient languages, such as Greek, Hebrew, and Syriac, as well as modern languages, such as

French and German. He added these to his knowledge of Italian and of Latin, which was once spoken fluently by all clerics and by all cultured people.

Thanks to his mastery of so many languages, Lawrence was able to carry out a busy apostolate among the different categories of people. As an effective preacher, his knowledge, not only of the Bible but also of the rabbinic literature, was so profound that even the Rabbis, impressed and full of admiration, treated him with esteem and respect. As a theologian steeped in Sacred Scripture and in the Fathers of the Church, he was also able to illustrate Catholic doctrine in an exemplary manner to Christians who, especially in Germany, had adhered to the Reformation. With his calm, clear exposition, he demonstrated the biblical and patristic foundation of all the articles of faith disputed by Martin Luther. These included the primacy of Saint Peter and of his Successors, the divine origin of the Episcopate, justification as an inner transformation of man, and the need to do good works for salvation. Lawrence's success helps us to realize that today, too, in pursuing ecumenical dialogue with such great hope, the reference to Sacred Scripture, interpreted in accordance with the Tradition of the Church, is an indispensable element of fundamental importance. I wished to recall this in my Apostolic Exhortation *Verbum Domini* (no. 46).

Even the simplest members of the faithful, those not endowed with great culture, benefited from the convincing words of Lawrence, who addressed humble people to remind them all to make their lives consistent with the faith they professed. This was a great merit of the Capuchins and of other religious orders which, in the sixteenth and seventeenth centuries, contributed to the renewal of Christian life, penetrating the depths of society with their witness of life and their teaching. Today, too, the new evangelization stands in need of well-trained apostles, zealous and courageous, so that the light and beauty of the Gospel may prevail over the cultural tendencies of ethical relativism and religious indifference and transform the various ways of thinking and acting into genuine Christian humanism. It is surprising that Saint Lawrence of Brindisi was able to continue without interruption his work as an appreciated and unflagging preacher in many cities of Italy and in different countries in spite of holding other burdensome offices of great responsibility. Indeed, within the Order of Capuchins he was professor of theology, novice master, several times provincial minister and definitor general, and finally, from 1602 to 1605, minister general.

In the midst of this mountain of work, Lawrence cultivated an exceptionally fervent spiritual life. He devoted much time to prayer and, especially, to the celebration of Holy Mass—often protracted for hours—caught up in and moved by the memorial of the Passion, death, and Resurrection of the Lord. At the school of the saints, every priest, as was emphasized frequently during the recent Year for Priests, may avoid the danger of activism—acting, that is, without remembering the profound motives of his ministry—only if he attends to his own inner life. In speaking to priests and seminarians in the Cathedral of Brindisi, Saint Lawrence's birthplace, I recalled that "the time he spends in prayer is the most important time in a priest's life, in which divine grace acts with greater effectiveness, making his ministry fruitful. The first service to render to the community is prayer. And, therefore, time for prayer must be given true priority in our life. . . . If we are not interiorly in communion with God, we cannot even give anything to others. Therefore, God is the first priority. We must always reserve the time necessary to be in communion of prayer with our Lord" (*Address of Benedict* XVI *to priests, deacons, and seminarians of the Archdiocese of Brindisi*, Cathedral of Brindisi, 15 June 2008). Moreover, with the unmistakable ardor of his style, Lawrence urged everyone, and not only priests, to cultivate a life of prayer, for it is through prayer that we speak to God and that God speaks to us: "Oh, if we were to consider this reality!" he exclaimed. "In other words, that God is truly present to us when we speak to him in prayer; that he truly listens to our prayers, even if we pray only with our hearts and minds. And that not only is he present and hears us, indeed, he willingly and with the greatest of pleasure wishes to grant our requests."

Another trait that characterizes the opus of this son of Saint Francis is his action for peace. Time and again both Supreme Pontiffs and Catholic Princes entrusted him with important diplomatic missions, to settle controversies and to encourage harmony among the European States, threatened in those days by the Ottoman Empire. The moral authority he enjoyed made him a counselor both sought after and listened to. Today, as in the times of Saint Lawrence, the world is in great need of peace, it needs peaceful and peacemaking men and women. All who believe in God must always be sources and artisans of peace. It was precisely on the occasion of one of these diplomatic missions that Lawrence's earthly life ended, in 1619 in Lisbon, where he had gone to see King Philip III of Spain to plead the cause of the Neapolitan subjects oppressed by the local authorities.

He was canonized in 1881, and his vigorous and intense activity, his vast and harmonious knowledge, earned him the title of *Doctor Apostolicus*, "Apostolic Doctor". The title was conferred on him by Blessed Pope John XXIII in 1959, on the occasion of the fourth centenary of his birth. This recognition was also granted to Lawrence of Brindisi because he was the author of numerous works of biblical exegesis, theology, and sermons. In them he offers an organic presentation of the history of salvation, centered on the mystery of the Incarnation, the greatest expression of divine love for mankind. Furthermore, since he was a highly qualified Mariologist, the author of a collection of sermons on Our Lady entitled *Mariale*, he highlighted the unique role of the Virgin Mary, whose Immaculate Conception and whose role in the redemption brought about by Christ he clearly affirms. With a fine theological sensitivity, Lawrence of Brindisi also pointed out the Holy Spirit's action in the believer's life. He reminds us that the Third Person of the Most Holy Trinity illumines and assists us with his gifts in our commitment to live joyously the Gospel message. "The Holy Spirit", Saint Lawrence wrote, "sweetens the yoke of the divine law and lightens its weight, so that we may observe God's commandments with the greatest of ease and even with pleasure."

I would like to complete this brief presentation of the life and doctrine of Saint Lawrence of Brindisi by underlining that the whole of his activity was inspired by great love for Sacred Scripture, which he knew thoroughly and by heart, and by the conviction that listening to and the reception of the word of God produces an inner transformation that leads us to holiness. "The word of the Lord", he said, "is a light for the mind and a fire for the will, so that man may know and love God. For the inner man, who lives through the living grace of God's Spirit, it is bread and water, but bread sweeter than honey and water better than wine or milk. . . . It is a weapon against a heart stubbornly entrenched in vice. It is a sword against the flesh, the world, and the devil, to destroy every sin." Saint Lawrence of Brindisi teaches us to love Sacred Scripture, to increase in familiarity with it, to cultivate daily relations of friendship with the Lord in prayer, so that our every action, our every activity, may have its beginning and its fulfillment in him. This is the source from which to draw so that our Christian witness may be luminous and able to lead the people of our time to God.

34

Saint Alphonsus Liguori

WEDNESDAY, 30 MARCH 2011
Saint Peter's Square

Dear Brothers and Sisters,

Today I would like to present to you the figure of a holy Doctor of the Church to whom we are deeply indebted because he was an outstanding moral theologian and a teacher of spiritual life for all, especially simple people. He is the author of the words and music of one of the most popular Christmas carols in Italy, and not only Italy: *Tu scendi dalle stelle* [You come down from the stars].

Belonging to a rich noble family of Naples, Alfonso Maria de' Liguori [known in English as Alphonsus Liguori] was born in 1696. Endowed with outstanding intellectual qualities, when he was only sixteen years old he obtained a degree in civil and canon law. He was the most brilliant lawyer in the tribunal of Naples: for eight years he won all the cases he defended. However, in his soul, thirsting for God and desirous of perfection, Alphonsus was led by the Lord to understand that he was calling him to a different vocation. In fact, in 1723, indignant at the corruption and injustice that was ruining the legal milieu, he abandoned his profession—and with it, riches and success—and decided to become a priest despite the opposition of his father. He had excellent teachers who introduced him to the study of Sacred Scripture, of Church history, and of mysticism. He acquired a vast theological culture which he put to good use when, after a few years, he embarked on his work as a writer. He was ordained a priest in 1726 and, for the exercise of his ministry, entered the diocesan Congregation of Apostolic Missions.

Alphonsus began an activity of evangelization and catechesis among the humblest classes of Neapolitan society, to whom he liked preaching and whom he instructed in the basic truths of the faith. Many of these people, poor and modest, to whom he addressed himself were very often prone to vice and involved in crime. He patiently taught them to pray, encouraging them to improve their way of life. Alphonsus obtained excellent results: in the most wretched districts of the city, there were an increasing number of groups that would meet in the evenings in private houses and workshops to pray and meditate on the word of God, under the guidance of several catechists trained by Alphonsus and by other priests, who regularly visited these groups of the faithful. When, at the wish of the Archbishop of Naples, these meetings were held in the chapels of the city, they came to be known as "evening chapels". They were a true and proper source of moral education, of social improvement, and of reciprocal help among the poor: thefts, duels, prostitution ended by almost disappearing.

Even though the social and religious context of the time of Saint Alphonsus was very different from our own, the "evening chapels" appear as a model of missionary action from which we may draw inspiration today, too, for a "new evangelization", particularly of the poorest people, and for building a more just, fraternal, and supportive coexistence. Priests were entrusted with a task of spiritual ministry, while well-trained lay people could be effective Christian animators, an authentic Gospel leaven in the midst of society. After having considered leaving to evangelize the pagan peoples, when Alphonsus was thirty-five years old, he came into contact with the peasants and shepherds of the hinterland of the Kingdom of Naples. Struck by their ignorance of religion and the state of neglect in which they were living, he decided to leave the capital and to dedicate himself to these people, poor both spiritually and materially. In 1732, he founded the religious Congregation of the Most Holy Redeemer, which he put under the protection of Bishop Tommaso Falcoia and of which he subsequently became the superior. These religious, guided by Alphonsus, were authentic itinerant missionaries, who also reached the most remote villages, exhorting people to convert and to persevere in the Christian life, especially through prayer. Still today, the Redemptorists, scattered in so many of the world's countries, with new forms of apostolate continue this mission of evangelization. I think of them with gratitude, urging them to be ever faithful to the example of their holy Founder.

Esteemed for his goodness and for his pastoral zeal, in 1762 Alphonsus was appointed Bishop of Sant'Agata dei Goti, a ministry which he left, following the illness which debilitated him, in 1775, through a concession of Pope Pius VI. On learning of his death in 1787, which occurred after great suffering, the Pontiff exclaimed: "he was a saint!" And he was not mistaken: Alphonsus was canonized in 1839, and in 1871 he was declared a Doctor of the Church. This title suited him for many reasons. First of all, because he offered a rich teaching of moral theology, which adequately expressed Catholic doctrine, to the point that Pope Pius XII proclaimed him "Patron of all confessors and moral theologians". In his day, there was a very strict and widespread interpretation of moral life because of the Jansenist mentality which, instead of fostering trust and hope in God's mercy, fomented fear and presented a grim and severe face of God, very remote from the face revealed to us by Jesus. Especially in his main work, entitled *Moral Theology*, Saint Alphonsus proposed a balanced and convincing synthesis of the requirements of God's law, engraved on our hearts, fully revealed by Christ and interpreted authoritatively by the Church, and of the dynamics of the conscience and of human freedom, which precisely in adherence to truth and goodness permit the person's development and fulfillment. Alphonsus recommended to pastors of souls and confessors that they be faithful to Catholic moral doctrine, assuming at the same time a charitable, understanding, and gentle attitude so that penitents might feel accompanied, supported, and encouraged on their journey of faith and of Christian life. Saint Alphonsus never tired of repeating that priests are a visible sign of the infinite mercy of God, who forgives and enlightens the mind and heart of the sinner so that he may convert and change his life. In our epoch, in which there are clear signs of the loss of the moral conscience and—it must be recognized—of a certain lack of esteem for the sacrament of confession, Saint Alphonsus' teaching is still very timely.

Together with theological works, Saint Alphonsus wrote many other works, destined for the religious formation of the people. His style is simple and pleasing. Read and translated into many languages, the works of Saint Alphonsus have contributed to molding the popular spirituality of the last two centuries. Some of the texts can be read with profit today, too, such as *The Eternal Maxims*, the *Glories of Mary*, *The Practice of Loving Jesus Christ*, which latter work is the synthesis of his thought and his masterpiece. He stressed the need for prayer, which enables one to open oneself to divine grace in order to do God's will every day and to obtain one's own sanctification. With regard to prayer, he writes: "God does not deny anyone the grace of prayer, with which one obtains help to overcome every form of concupiscence and every temptation. And I say, and I will always repeat as long as I live, that the whole of our salvation lies in prayer." Hence his famous axiom: "He who prays is saved" (*Del gran mezzo della preghiera e opuscoli affini. Opere ascetiche* II, Rome, 1962, p. 171). In this regard, an exhortation of my Predecessor, the Venerable Servant of God John Paul II, comes to mind. "Our Christian communities must become genuine 'schools' of prayer.... It is therefore essential that education in prayer should become in some way a key-point of all pastoral planning" (Apostolic Letter *Novo Millennio Ineunte*, nos. 33, 34).

Among the forms of prayer fervently recommended by Saint Alphonsus stands out the visit to the Blessed Sacrament, or, as we would call it today, "adoration", brief or extended, personal or as a community, before the Eucharist. "Certainly", Saint Alphonsus writes, "amongst all devotions, after that of receiving the sacraments, that of adoring Jesus in the Blessed Sacrament takes the first place, is the most pleasing to God and the most useful to ourselves.... Oh, what a beautiful delight to be before an altar with faith ... to represent our wants to him, as a friend does to a friend in whom he places all his trust" (*Visits to the Most Blessed Sacrament and to the Blessed Virgin Mary for Each Day of the Month. Introduction*). Alphonsian spirituality is in fact eminently Christological, centered on Christ and on his Gospel. Meditation on the mystery of the Incarnation and on the Lord's Passion were often the subject of Saint Alphonsus' preaching. In these events, in fact, redemption is offered to all human beings "in abundance". And precisely because it is Christological, Alphonsian piety is also exquisitely Marian. Deeply devoted to Mary, he illustrates her role in the history of salvation: an associate in the redemption and Mediatrix of grace, Mother, Advocate, and Queen. In addition, Saint Alphonsus states that devotion to Mary will be of great comfort to us at the moment of our death. He was convinced that meditation on our eternal destiny, on our call to participate forever in the beatitude of God as well as on the tragic possibility of damnation, contributes to living with serenity and dedication and to facing the reality of death, ever preserving full trust in God's goodness.

Saint Alphonsus Maria Liguori is an example of a zealous Pastor who conquered souls by preaching the Gospel and administering the sacraments combined with behavior impressed with gentle and merciful goodness that was born from his intense relationship with God, who is infinite Goodness. He had a realistically optimistic vision of the resources of good that the Lord gives to every person, and he gave importance to the affections and sentiments of the heart, as well as to the mind, in order to be able to love God and neighbor. To conclude, I would like to recall that our Saint, like Saint Francis de Sales—of whom I spoke a few weeks ago—insists that holiness is accessible to every Christian: "the religious as a religious; the secular as a secular; the priest as a priest; the married as married; the man of business as a man of business; the soldier as a soldier; and so of every other state of life" (*Practica di amare Gesù Cristo. Opere ascetiche I* [*The Practice of the Love of Jesus Christ*, Ascetic Works 1], Rome, 1933, p. 79). Let us thank the Lord, who with his Providence inspired saints and Doctors in different times and places, who speak the same language to invite us to grow in faith and to live with love and with joy our being Christians in the simple everyday actions, to walk on the path of holiness, on the path toward God and toward true joy.

35

Saint Thérèse of Lisieux

WEDNESDAY, 6 APRIL 2011
Saint Peter's Square

Dear Brothers and Sisters,

Today I would like to talk to you about Saint Thérèse of Lisieux, Thérèse of the Child Jesus and of the Holy Face, who lived in this world for only twenty-four years, at the end of the nineteenth century, leading a very simple and hidden life, but who, after her death and the publication of her writings, became one of the best-known and best-loved saints. "Little Thérèse" has never stopped helping the simplest souls, the little, the poor, and the suffering who pray to her. However, she has also illumined the whole Church with her profound spiritual doctrine to the point that Venerable Pope John Paul II chose, in 1997, to give her the title "Doctor of the Church", in addition to that of Patroness of Missions, which Pius XI had already attributed to her in 1939. My beloved Predecessor described her as an "expert in the *scientia amoris*" (*Novo Millennio Ineunte*, no. 42). Thérèse expressed this science, in which she saw the whole truth of the faith shine out in love, mainly in the *story of her life*, published a year after her death with the title *Story of a Soul*. The book immediately met with enormous success; it was translated into many languages and disseminated throughout the world. I would like to invite you to rediscover this small-great treasure, this luminous comment on the Gospel lived to the full! *The Story of a Soul*, in fact, is a marvelous *story of Love*, told with such authenticity, simplicity, and freshness that the reader cannot but be fascinated by it! But what was this Love that filled Thérèse's whole life, from childhood to death? Dear friends, this Love has a Face, it has a Name, it is Jesus! The Saint speaks continuously of Jesus. Let us therefore review the important stages of her life, to enter into the heart of her teaching.

Thérèse was born on 2 January 1873 in Alençon, a city in Normandy, in France. She was the last daughter of Louis and Zélie Martin, a married couple and exemplary parents, who were beatified together on 19 October 2008. They had nine children, four of whom died at a tender age. Five daughters were left, who all became religious. Thérèse, at the age of four, was deeply upset by the death of her mother (Ms A 13r). Her father then moved with his daughters to the town of Lisieux, where the Saint was to spend her whole life. Later Thérèse, affected by a serious nervous disorder, was healed by a divine grace which she herself described as the "smile of Our Lady" (*ibid.*, 29v–30v). She then received her First Communion, which was an intense experience (*ibid.*, 35r), and made Jesus in the Eucharist the center of her life.

The "grace of Christmas" of 1886 marked the important turning-point, which she called her "complete conversion" (*ibid.*, 44v–45r). In fact she recovered totally from her childhood hyper-sensitivity and began "to run as a giant". At the age of fourteen, Thérèse became ever closer, with great faith, to the Crucified Jesus. She took to heart the apparently desperate case of a criminal sentenced to death who was impenitent. "I wanted at all costs to prevent him from going to hell", the Saint wrote, convinced that her prayers would put him in touch with the redeeming Blood of Jesus. It was her first and fundamental experience of *spiritual motherhood*: "I had such great trust in the Infinite Mercy of Jesus", she wrote. Together with Mary Most Holy, young Thérèse loved, believed, and hoped with "a mother's heart" (cf. Pr 6/10r).

In November 1887, Thérèse went on pilgrimage to Rome with her father and her sister Céline (*ibid.*, 55v–67r). The culminating moment for her was the Audience with Pope Leo XIII, whom she asked for permission to enter the Carmel of Lisieux when she was only just fifteen. A year later her wish was granted. She became a Carmelite, "to save souls and to pray for priests" (*ibid.*, 69v). At the same time, her father began to suffer from a painful and humiliating mental illness. It caused Thérèse great suffering, which led her to contemplation of the Face of Jesus in his Passion (*ibid.*, 71rv). Thus, her name as a religious—*Sister Thérèse of the Child Jesus and of the Holy Face*—expresses the program of her whole life in communion with the central mysteries of the Incarnation and the redemption. Her religious profession, on the Feast of the Nativity of Mary, 8 September 1890, was a true spiritual espousal in evangelical "littleness", characterized by the symbol of the flower: "It was the Nativity of Mary. What a beautiful feast on which to become the Spouse of Jesus! It was the *little* new-born Holy Virgin who presented her *little* Flower to the *little* Jesus" (*ibid.*, 77r). For Thérèse, being a religious meant being a *bride of Jesus and a mother of souls* (cf. Ms B, 2v). On the same day, the Saint wrote a prayer which expressed the entire orientation of her life: she asked Jesus for the gift of his infinite Love, to be the smallest, and above all she asked for the salvation of all human beings: "That no soul may be damned today" (Pr 2). Of great importance is her *Offering to Merciful Love*, made on the Feast of the Most Holy Trinity in 1895 (Ms A, 83v–84r; Pr 6). It was an offering that Thérèse immediately shared with her sisters, since she was already acting novice mistress.

Ten years after the "grace of Christmas" in 1896 came the "grace of Easter", which opened the last period of Thérèse's life with the beginning of her passion in profound union with the Passion of Jesus. It was the passion of her body, with the illness that led to her death through great suffering, but it was especially the passion of the soul, with a very painful *trial of faith* (Ms C, 4v–7v). With Mary beside the Cross of Jesus, Thérèse then lived the most heroic faith, as a light in the darkness that invaded her soul. The Carmelite was aware that she was living this great trial for the salvation of all the atheists of the modern world, whom she called "brothers". She then lived fraternal love even more intensely (8r–33v): for the sisters of her community, for her two spiritual missionary brothers, for the priests, and for all people, especially the most distant. She truly became a "universal sister"! Her lovable, smiling charity was the expression of the profound joy whose secret she reveals: "Jesus, my joy is loving you" (P 45/7). In this context of suffering, living the greatest love in the smallest things of daily life, the Saint brought to fulfillment her vocation to be Love in the heart of the Church (cf. Ms B, 3v).

Thérèse died on the evening of 30 September 1897, saying the simple words, "My God, I love you!" looking at the Crucifix she held tightly in her hands. These last words of the Saint are the key to her whole doctrine, to her interpretation of the Gospel. The act of love, expressed in her last breath was, as it were, the continuous breathing of her soul, the beating of her heart. The simple words "*Jesus I love you*" are at the heart of all her writings. The act of love for Jesus immersed her in the Most Holy Trinity. She wrote: "Ah, you know, Divine Jesus I love you / The spirit of Love enflames me with his fire, / It is in loving you that I attract the Father" (P 17/2).

Dear friends, we too, with Saint Thérèse of the Child Jesus, must be able to repeat to the Lord every day that we want to live of love for him and for others, to learn at the school of the saints to love authentically and totally. Thérèse is one of the "little" ones of the Gospel who let themselves be led by God to the depths of his mystery. A guide for all, especially those who, in the People of God, carry out their ministry as theologians. With humility and charity, faith and hope, Thérèse continually entered the heart of Sacred Scripture, which contains the mystery of Christ. And this interpretation of the Bible, nourished by the *science of love*, is not in opposition to academic knowledge. The *science of the saints*, in fact, of which she herself speaks on the last page of her *Story of a Soul*, is the loftiest science. "All the saints have understood and in a special way perhaps those who fill the universe with the radiance of the evangelical doctrine. Was it not from prayer that Saint Paul, Saint Augustine, Saint John of the Cross, Saint Thomas Aquinas, Francis, Dominic, and so many other friends of God drew that *wonderful science* which has enthralled the loftiest minds?" (cf. Ms C, 36r). Inseparable from the Gospel, for Thérèse the Eucharist was the sacrament of Divine Love that stoops to the extreme to raise us to him. In her last *Letter*, on an image that represents the Child Jesus in the consecrated Host, the Saint wrote these simple words: "I cannot fear a God who made himself so small for me! . . . I love him! In fact, he is nothing but Love and Mercy!" (LT 266).

In the Gospel, Thérèse discovered above all the Mercy of Jesus, to the point that she said: "To me, he has given his Infinite Mercy, and it is in this ineffable mirror that I contemplate his other divine attributes. Therein all appear to me radiant with Love. His Justice, even more perhaps than the rest, seems to me to be clothed with Love" (Ms A, 84r). In these words, she expresses herself in the last lines of *Story of a Soul*: "I have only to open the Holy Gospels, and at once I breathe the perfume of Jesus' life, and then I know which way to run; and it is not to the first place, but to the last, that I hasten. . . . I feel that even had I on my conscience every crime one could commit . . . my heart broken with sorrow, I would throw myself into the arms of my Savior Jesus, because I know that he loves the Prodigal Son" who returns to him (Ms C, 36v–37r). "Trust and Love" are therefore the final point of the account of her life, two words, like beacons, that illumined the whole of her journey to holiness, to be able to guide others on the same "little way of trust and love", of spiritual childhood (cf. Ms C, 2v–3r; LT 226). Trust, like that of the child who abandons himself in God's hands, inseparable from the strong, radical commitment of true love, which is the total gift of self forever, as the Saint says, contemplating Mary: "Loving is giving all, and giving oneself" (*Why I Love Thee, Mary*, P 54/22). Thus Thérèse points out to us all that Christian life consists in living to the full the grace of baptism in the total gift of self to the Love of the Father, in order to live like Christ, in the fire of the Holy Spirit, his same love for all others.

36

Holiness

WEDNESDAY, 13 APRIL 2011
Saint Peter's Square

Dear Brothers and Sisters,

At the General Audiences in the past two years we have been accompanied by the figures of so many saints: we have learned to know them more closely and to understand that the whole of the Church's history is marked by these men and women who with their faith, with their charity, and with their life have been beacons for so many generations, as they are for us, too. The saints expressed in various ways the powerful and transforming presence of the Risen One. They let Jesus so totally overwhelm their life that they could say with Saint Paul, "it is no longer I who live, but Christ who lives in me" (Gal 2:20). Following their example, seeking their intercession, entering into communion with them, "brings us closer to Christ, so our companionship with the saints joins us to Christ, from whom as from their fountain and head issue every grace and the life of the People of God itself" (cf. Second Vatican Council, Dogmatic Constitution on the Church, *Lumen Gentium*, no. 50).

At the end of this series of Catecheses, therefore, I would like to offer some thoughts on what holiness is. What does it mean to be holy? Who is called to be holy? We are often led to think that holiness is a goal reserved for a few elect. Saint Paul, instead, speaks of God's great plan and says: "even as he (God) chose us in him [Christ] before the foundation of the world, that we should be holy and blameless before him" (Eph 1:4). And he was speaking about all of us. At the center of the divine plan is Christ, in whom God shows his Face, in accord with the favor of his will. The mystery hidden in the centuries is revealed in its fullness in the Word made flesh. And Paul then says: "in him all the fullness of God was pleased to dwell" (Col 1:19). In Christ the living God made himself close, visible, audible, and tangible so that each one might draw from his fullness of grace and truth (cf. Jn 1:14–16). Therefore, the whole of Christian life knows one supreme law, which Saint Paul expresses in a formula that recurs in all his holy writings: in Jesus Christ. Holiness, the fullness of Christian life, does not consist in carrying out extraordinary enterprises but in being united with Christ, in living his mysteries, in making our own his example, his thoughts, his behavior. The measure of holiness stems from the stature that Christ achieves in us, in as much as with the power of the Holy Spirit, we model our whole life on his. It is being conformed to Jesus, as Saint Paul says: "For those whom he foreknew he also predestined to be conformed to the image of his Son" (Rom 8:29). And Saint Augustine exclaimed: "my life shall be a real life, being wholly filled by you" (*Confessions* 10, XXVIII). The Second Vatican Council, in the Dogmatic Constitution on the Church, speaks with clarity of the universal call to holiness, saying that no one is excluded: "The forms and tasks of life are many, but holiness is one—that sanctity which is cultivated by all who act under God's Spirit and . . . follow Christ, poor, humble, and cross-bearing, that they may deserve to be partakers of his glory" (*Lumen Gentium*, no. 41).

However, the question remains: how can we take the path to holiness, in order to respond to this call? Can I do this on my own initiative? The answer is clear. A holy life is not primarily the result of our efforts, of our actions, because it is God, the three times Holy (cf. Is 6:3), who sanctifies us, it is the Holy Spirit's action that enlivens us from within, it is the very life of the Risen Christ that is communicated to us and that transforms us. To say so once again with the Second Vatican Council, "the followers of Christ, called by God, not in virtue of their works, but by his design and grace and justified in the Lord Jesus, have been made sons of God in the baptism of faith and partakers of the divine nature and so are truly sanctified. They must therefore hold onto and perfect in their lives that sanctification which they have received" (*ibid.*, no. 40). Holiness, therefore, has its deepest root in the grace of baptism, in being grafted on to the Paschal Mystery of Christ, by which his Spirit is communicated to us, his very life as the Risen One. Saint Paul strongly emphasizes the transformation that baptismal grace brings about in man, and he reaches the point of coining a new terminology, forged with the preposition "with": *dead-with, buried-with, raised-with*, brought to *life-with*, with Christ; our destiny is indissolubly linked to his. "We were buried therefore with him by baptism", he writes, "into death, so that as Christ was raised from the dead . . . we too might walk in newness of life" (Rom 6:4). Yet God always respects our freedom and asks that we accept this gift and live the requirements it entails, and he asks that we let ourselves be transformed by the action of the Holy Spirit, conforming our will to the will of God.

How can it happen that our manner of thinking and our actions become thinking and action with Christ and of Christ? What is the soul of holiness? Once again the

Second Vatican Council explains; it tells us that Christian holiness is nothing other than charity lived to the full. "God is love, and he who abides in love abides in God, and God abides in him" (1 Jn 4:16). Now

> God has poured out his love in our hearts through the Holy Spirit who has been given to us (cf. Rom 5:5); therefore the first and most necessary gift is charity, by which we love God above all things and our neighbor through love of him. But if charity, like a good seed, is to grow and fructify in the soul, each of the faithful must willingly hear the word of God and carry out his will with deeds, with the help of his grace. He must frequently receive the sacraments, chiefly the Eucharist, and take part in the holy liturgy; he must constantly apply himself to prayer, self-denial, active brotherly service, and the exercise of all the virtues. This is because love, as the bond of perfection and fullness of the law (cf. Col 3:14; Rom 13:10), governs, gives meaning to, and perfects all the means of sanctification. (cf. *Lumen Gentium*, no. 42)

Perhaps this language of the Second Vatican Council is a little too solemn for us; perhaps we should say things even more simply. What is the essential? The essential means never leaving a Sunday without an encounter with the Risen Christ in the Eucharist; this is not an additional burden but is light for the whole week. It means never beginning and never ending a day without at least a brief contact with God. And, on the path of our life it means following the "signposts" that God has communicated to us in the Ten Commandments, interpreted with Christ, which are merely the explanation of what love is in specific situations. It seems to me that this is the true simplicity and greatness of a life of holiness: the encounter with the Risen One on Sunday; contact with God at the beginning and at the end of the day; following, in decisions, the "signposts" that God has communicated to us, which are but forms of charity. "Hence the true disciple of Christ is marked by love both of God and of neighbor" (*Lumen Gentium*, no. 42). This is the true simplicity, greatness, and depth of Christian life, of being holy.

This is why Saint Augustine, in commenting on the fourth chapter of the First Letter of Saint John, could make a bold statement: "*Dilige et fac quod vis* [Love and do what you will]." And he continued: "If you keep silent, keep silent by love: if you speak, speak by love; if you correct, correct by love; if you pardon, pardon by love; let love be rooted in you, and from the root nothing but good can grow" (7, 8: PL 35). Those who are guided by love, who live charity to the full, are guided by God, because God is love. Hence these important words apply: "*Dilige et fac quod vis*", "Love and do what you will."

We might ask ourselves: can we, with our limitations, with our weaknesses, aim so high? During the Liturgical Year, the Church invites us to commemorate a host of saints, the ones, that is, who lived charity to the full, who knew how to love and follow Christ in their daily lives. They tell us that it is possible for everyone to take this road. In every epoch of the Church's history, on every latitude of the world map, the saints belong to all the ages and to every state of life; they are actual faces of every people, language, and nation. And they have very different characters. Actually I must say that also for my personal faith many saints, not all, are true stars in the firmament of history. And I would like to add that for me not only a few great saints whom I love and whom I know well are "signposts", but precisely also the simple saints, that is, the good people I see in my life who will never be canonized. They are ordinary people, so to speak, without visible heroism, but in their everyday goodness I see the truth of faith. This goodness, which they have developed in the faith of the Church, is for me the most reliable apology of Christianity and the sign of where the truth lies.

In the Communion of Saints, canonized and not canonized, which the Church lives, thanks to Christ, in all her members, we enjoy their presence and their company and cultivate the firm hope that we shall be able to imitate their journey and share one day in the same blessed life, eternal life.

Dear friends, how great and beautiful as well as simple is the Christian vocation seen in this light! We are all called to holiness: it is the very measure of Christian living. Once again Saint Paul expresses it with great intensity when he writes: "grace was given to each of us according to the measure of Christ's gift. . . . His gifts were that some should be apostles, some prophets, some evangelists, some pastors and teachers, to equip the saints for the work of ministry, for building up the body of Christ, until we all attain to the unity of the faith and of the knowledge of the Son of God, to mature manhood, to the measure of the stature of the fullness of Christ" (Eph 4:7, 11–13). I would like to ask all to open themselves to the action of the Holy Spirit, who transforms our life, to be, we too, like small pieces in the great mosaic of holiness that God continues to create in history, so that the face of Christ may shine out in the fullness of its splendor. Let us not be afraid to aim high, for God's heights; let us not be afraid that God will ask too much of us, but let ourselves be guided by his Word in every daily action, even when we feel poor, inadequate, sinners. It will be he who transforms us in accordance with his love.